KU-253-824

UK Price
£4.95

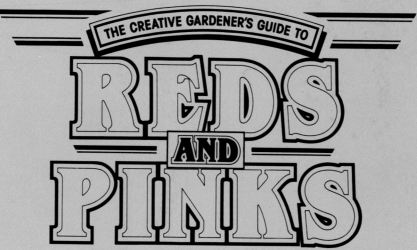

THE CREATIVE GARDENER'S GUIDE TO

REDS AND PINKS

How to mix and match over 100 stunning flowers, shrubs and trees
to create a garden of beauty

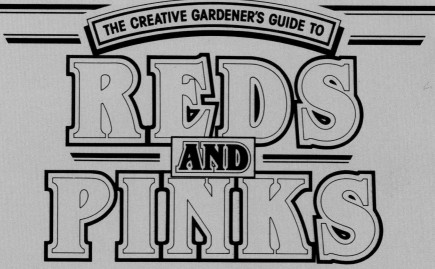

THE CREATIVE GARDENER'S GUIDE TO

REDS AND PINKS

How to mix and match over 100 stunning flowers, shrubs and trees
to create a garden of beauty

DAVID SQUIRE

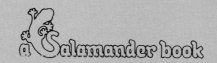

a Salamander book

Published by Salamander Books Limited
LONDON • NEW YORK

A SALAMANDER BOOK

CREDITS

© 1986 Salamander Books Ltd.,
52 Bedford Row,
London WC1R 4LR,
United Kingdom

ISBN 0 86101 222 4

Distributed in the UK by
Hodder & Stoughton Services,
P.O. Box 6, Mill Road, Dunton Green,
Sevenoaks, Kent TN13 2XX

All rights reserved. No part of this book may be reproduced, stored in a retrieval system, or transmitted in any form or by any means, electronic, mechanical, photocopying, recording or otherwise, without the prior permission of Salamander Books Ltd.

All correspondence concerning the content of this volume should be addressed to Salamander Books Ltd.

Author
David Squire brings to this series practical experience both as a gardener and holder of many horticultural awards (including the Wisley Diploma in Horticulture and the N.K. Gould Memorial Prize from the internationally famous Royal Horticultural Society at Wisley, Surrey) and as the author of 14 books on gardening. He still finds time to improve and enjoy the colourful garden at his home in West Sussex.

Editor
Jonathan Elphick

Designer
Barry Savage

Colour and monochrome reproductions
Melbourne Graphics Ltd, London, England

Filmset
Instep Print & Design Ltd, London, England

Printed in Belgium
by Proost International Book Production, Turnhout

CONTENTS

Introduction

HOW TO USE THIS BOOK

Gardeners are like painters, but with fresh canvas available to them only once a year. Borders are planned, plant and seed catalogues avidly searched and gleaned for more vibrant and longer-lasting colours, and fellow gardeners consulted. But should you or your family have a taste for certain colours — perhaps those that contrast with established plants in your garden, blend happily against colour-washed walls, or create memories of a cherished display in a wedding bouquet — then you need further help at your elbow. You need a reliable guide which clearly portrays the range of garden plants within a particular part of the colour spectrum, and that is the purpose of this lavishly illustrated all-colour book.

The introductory pages explain the nature of light and colour and how different colours are measured and defined, according to their hue, value and intensity. There is also useful information on the influence of shiny or matt surfaces, why some colours are dominant and the effects of bright sunlight and the shadows of evening. Planning colour with the aid of a *colour-circle* is fully covered, and the concept of complementary and harmonizing colours is discussed in detail.

The main section of this *Creative Gardener's Guide* consists of five chapters, detailing pink and red plants in a wide range of garden settings: filling annual and herbaceous borders, adorning rock and naturalized gardens, bringing colour to window-boxes, hanging baskets, troughs and other containers on patios and terraces, clothing bare walls, climbing trellises or serving as a harmonious framework to knit together the various elements of your garden design. Each plant is illustrated in full colour and clearly described, including its botanical and common names, height and spread (in metric and imperial units), cultivation and propagation. Within each chapter the plants are arranged alphabetically according to their botanical names. At the base of each page there are valuable tips on using combinations of plants to create colour-contrasts, subtle harmonies, focal points and interesting shapes and patterns. Flowers suitable for home decoration are also mentioned.

At the end of the book there are two comprehensive indexes. The first lists all common names, indicating if they are used in the British Isles or the United States. The second index is of botanical names, including synonyms (alternative names). The inclusion of the latter helps you identify plants botanists have recently re-classified and given new names, which are frequently sold under their old, better-known names.

This book forms part of the successful series of *Creative Gardener's Guides* and is designed to help bring further colour and interest to all gardens, whatever their size and wherever they are. Other books in this all-colour series detail the uses of *Golds and Yellows*, *Blues and Purples*, and *Whites and Silvers*, while further gardening dimensions are revealed in the *Scented Garden* and the *Variegated Garden*. Each book forms a comprehensive and concise guide to a particular range of colours or garden theme, but when formed into a colour library can benefit garden planning in a manner few other books have ever achieved.

Above: **Malus x purpurea 'Lemoinei'**
This small deciduous tree with deep wine-red flowers creates a bold display that will suit most gardens, whether large or small.

Above: **Rhus typhina**
This tree from North America creates a blaze of colour throughout autumn. The leaves turn from vivid yellow through fiery reds to purple.

Key:
1 *Juniperus chinensis* 'Pyramidalis'
2 *Fuchsia magellanica* 'Aurea'
3 *Papaver orientale* 'Mrs Perry'
4 *Clematis* 'Nelly Moser'
5 *Thymus drucei* 'Annie Hall'
6 Mixture of geraniums
7 *Helianthemum nummularium* 'Raspberry Ripple'
8 Trailing lobelia, petunias, nasturtiums, geraniums and marigolds
9 Geranium 'Harlequin'
10 *Petunia* 'Honeybunch'
11 *Alcea rosea* (Hollyhock)

Introduction

THE SCIENCE OF COLOUR EVALUATION

What are light and colour?

The vast range of colours we see in our gardens and homes, with their near infinite subtleties of quality, shades of light as well as intensity, can be accurately measured. But what exactly are light and colour? To state coldly and scientifically that they are forms of electromagnetic radiation clearly disregards their beauty, but, technically speaking, that is their nature.

Electromagnetic radiation comes from the sun, and its range is wide, from gamma rays to low-frequency radio waves. But only a very small part of this extensive spectrum is in the form of visible light, from wavelengths at around 0.0004mm when the colour is deep violet, through blue, green, yellow, orange and red to deep red, with a wavelength of 0.0007mm. The wavelengths of red light range from 0.000723 to 0.000647mm.
See Diagram 1, below.

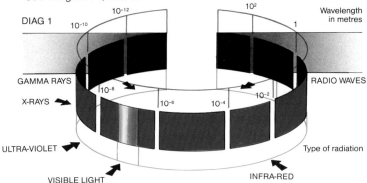

DIAG 2

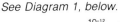

DIAG 1

Defining colour

Colours can be conceived as having three dimensions — *hue, value* and *intensity*.

Hue
This first dimension is the quality by which colours are basically distinguished one from another, such as yellow from red, green, blue or purple. For convenience, the colours so defined are those that are easily recognized, such as red, yellow, green, blue and violet. However, the Munsell System in North America defines the principal hues as red, yellow, green, blue and purple, with intermediate ones as yellow-red, green-yellow, blue-green, purple-blue and red-purple. In reality these names do no more than define points in a continuous range of hues that form a transitional and continuous band of colour. They are best conceived as a circle of pure colour, containing no white, grey or black whatsoever.

If a strip of paper with ten equal divisions is marked and coloured with the five principal and five intermediate hues of the Munsell System and held in a circle the continuous range of hues and their relationship one to another can be seen.
See Diagram 2, top right.

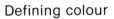

DIAG 3

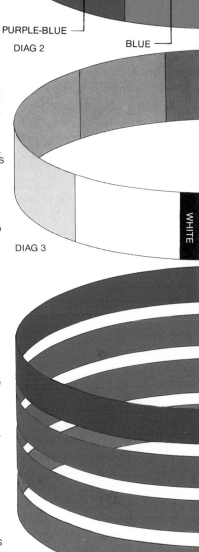

DIAG 4

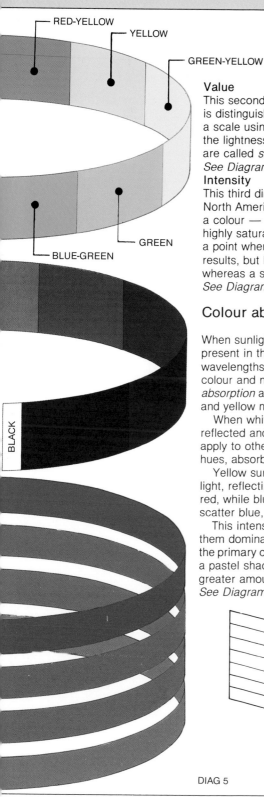

RED-YELLOW

YELLOW

GREEN-YELLOW

GREEN

BLUE-GREEN

BLACK

Value

This second dimension defines the quality by which a light colour is distinguished from a dark one. This is most easily depicted on a scale using black and white as the extremes. When defining the lightness or darkness within a colour, those with dark colours are called *shades*, while those that are light are *tints*.
See Diagram 3, centre left.

Intensity

This third dimension is also known as *saturation* or *purity*, and in North America as *chroma*. It defines the strength or weakness of a colour — its brightness or greyness. For instance, red can be highly saturated with colour, or the pigments slowly decreased to a point when it becomes grey. Other colours will produce similar results, but light hues such as yellow will become light grey, whereas a stronger one like purple will become dark grey.
See Diagram 4, bottom left.

Colour absorption

When sunlight falls upon coloured surfaces a few of the colours present in the white light — which contains a mixture of all wavelengths of the visible spectrum — may be absorbed by the colour and not reflected. This process is known as *colour absorption* and tends to make primary hues such as red, blue and yellow more dominant.

When white light falls on a white surface, most of the rays are reflected and the subject appears white. This, however, does not apply to other surfaces. Red, the most colour saturated of all hues, absorbs green and blue light but reflects red.

Yellow surfaces absorb the blues, indigos and violets in white light, reflecting mainly yellow as well as some green, orange and red, while blue surfaces absorb red, orange and yellow rays, and scatter blue, together with green, indigo and violet.

This intensification of reds, blues and yellows tends to make them dominant. Fully saturated hues reflect no more than two of the primary colours, whereas pink, which is a desaturated red — a pastel shade — reflects all three of the primary colours but a greater amount of red.
See Diagram 5, below.

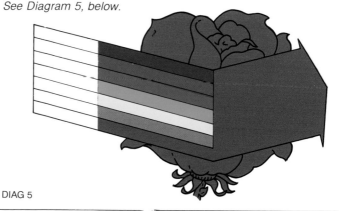

DIAG 5

Introduction

USING COLOUR IN THE GARDEN

Colour Wheels

Colour wheels are frequently used to aid colour planning in the garden. When the great English scientist Sir Isaac Newton investigated light in the late 1600s, he made a wheel formed of seven colours (red, orange, yellow, green, blue, indigo and violet). The American scientist A.H. Munsell in the second part of the 1800s researched colour assessment based on equal changes in the visual spectrum. He created a colour wheel formed of five principal colours (red, yellow, green, blue and purple, with intermediate ones between them). Other wheels have been created using four colours (red, yellow, green and blue).

However, the easiest colour circle to use is formed of three basic hues (red, yellow and blue) with three secondary ones (orange, green and violet). The secondary colours are created by overlapping the basic hues.

These colour circles indicate complementary colours (those diametrically opposite) and those that harmonize with each other (those in adjacent segments). Complementary hues are those with no common pigments, while harmonizing ones share the same pigments. Therefore, it can be seen that yellow and violet, blue and orange, red and green are complementary colours, while yellow harmonizes with green and orange, blue with green and violet, and red with orange and violet.

This colour-circle is formed by mixing coloured paints, by the process known as *subtractive colour mixing*. The other method of creating colour is by projecting three separate coloured lights (red, green and blue) onto a white surface. This process, known as *additive colour mixing*, creates colours with a different bias. *See Diagram 6, of a subtractive colour circle, below.*

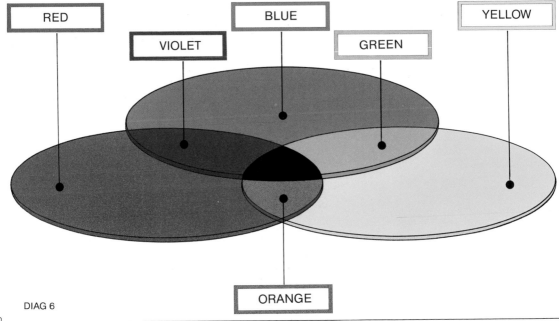

RED

VIOLET

BLUE

GREEN

YELLOW

ORANGE

DIAG 6

Below: **Celosia argentea plumosa 'Red Fox'**
This dark-leaved, maroon-flowered plant mixes well with yellow flowers.

Shiny and matt surfaces

The surface texture of a leaf, flower or stem influences the reflected light and its effect on the eye. A smooth surface reflects light at the same angle at which the light hits it. This makes the light purer in colour than the same light reflected from a matt surface. There, the irregularities of the surface scatter the reflected light and create an impression of dullness. Another effect of different surface texture is that smooth surfaces appear darker and matt ones lighter. In Nature, however, few plant surfaces are as smooth as glass, and the scattering of reflected light occurs from most of them.
See Diagram 7, below.

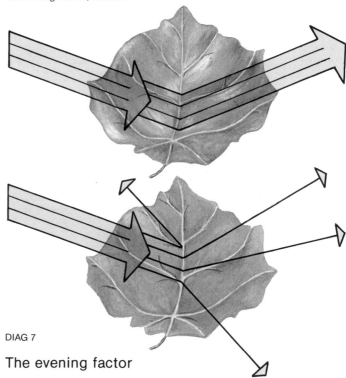

DIAG 7

The evening factor

The well-known delight of shepherds to have red sky at night, indicating a fine tomorrow, results from a clear sky as the sun's rays penetrate atmospheric particles and the air molecules themselves. Even though the sky appears blue, the rays become redder, because blue light is not created but scattered out of white light. This change to the violet end of the spectrum makes dark colours even darker. Saturated reds are made darker, while whites and yellows are not so dramatically affected. Pinks, because they are not totally saturated with colour, are not so affected as colour-intense reds. Conversely, bright sunshine glaring down at midday highlights light colours more than dark ones, such as saturated reds.

Above: **Cotoneaster lacteus**
The dense clusters of autumn and early winter berries are highlighted by the reflections from the shiny leaves surrounding them.

Introduction

HARMONIES AND CONTRASTS IN REDS AND PINKS

Reds are often the most dominant of all colours in a garden and in a totally colour-saturated form are exceptionally powerful and occasionally overpowering to the eye. When seen against a mid-green background, densely-red flowers, such as those of some poppies, have a three-dimensional effect and appear to stand out from the foliage and stems. Most red flowers, however, are not totally colour saturated and appear as shades. Pinks are desaturated reds, which means that they contain only a small proportion of red pigments.

Reds are available throughout the year, either as flower colours, in bright stems and barks, berries or as autumn colour. Even during winter many ericas, such as *Erica herbacea* (*E. carnea*) 'Ruby Glow' (rich dark red), *E. h.* 'Springwood Pink' (clear rose-pink) and *E. h.* 'Winter Beauty' (rose-pink) create welcome colour, and look good against colour-contrasting conifers.

Autumn-coloured trees featuring reds mixed with other colours present a dramatic display and focal point on a lawn during autumn. These include *Acer capillipes* with silvery-green striated bark, coral-red young growths and mid-green leaves that turn crimson in autumn; *Acer griseum*, the Paperbark Maple, a slow-growing tree with beautiful cinnamon-coloured underbark and trifoliate leaves turning red and scarlet in autumn; *Acer ginnala*, a bushy shrub with mid-green three-lobed leaves that become vivid crimson during autumn, but often for a short period only; *Liquidambar styraciflua*, the Sweet Gum, a large tree with five to seven-lobed shining dark green leaves that assume crimson and gold shades during autumn; *Prunus* 'Ukon', with semi-double cream to pale yellow flowers in late spring, followed in autumn by rusty-red leaves; *Prunus* 'Umineko', a narrow and upright tree with single white flowers during spring, followed by leaves tinted red and gold in autumn; *Prunus x hillieri* 'Spire', with a conical head and rich crimson leaves in autumn; *Prunus avium*, a vigorous tree with leaves red in autumn; and *Quercus coccinea*, the Scarlet Oak, which bears glossy mid-green leaves that turn scarlet in autumn. The form 'Splendens' has even redder leaves.

Coloured Barks and Stems

Many shrubs and trees have bark or stems with red tints, which can create lovely glowing effects, especially during winter. One of the best is *Acer platanoides* 'Schwedleri', a form of the Norway Maple with bronzy-red shoots. To produce these coloured growths the tree needs to be pruned hard every other autumn. *Prunus serrula* is a medium-sized tree grown mainly for its attractive bark, the outer part of which peels to reveal a polished, reddish-brown, mahogany-like layer. *Tilia platyphyllos* 'Rubra', the Red-twigged Lime, has a semi-erect growth habit with bright brownish-red shoots, especially attractive during winter. *Arbutus x andrachnoides* is stunningly attractive, with eye-catching cinnamon-red branches. Perhaps the best-known red-stemmed shrub is *Cornus alba*, the Red-barked Dogwood, and its many forms. *Salix alba* 'Chermesina', the Scarlet Willow, is dramatically conspicuous during winter, with orange-red branches and stems. Prune the tree severely every other year.

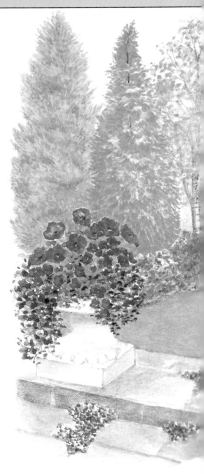

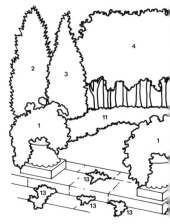

Key:
1 Trailing lobelias, petunias and late wallflowers
2 *Cupressus macrocarpa* 'Gold Crest'
3 *Chamaecyparis lawsoniana* 'Pembury Blue'
4 *Betula pendula* (Silver Birch)
5 *Chamaecyparis lawsoniana* 'Pottenii'

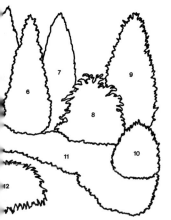

6 *Chamaecyparis lawsoniana* 'Lutea'
7 *Chamaecyparis lawsoniana* 'Allumii'
8 *Juniperus squamata* 'Meyeri'
9 *Chamaecyparis lawsoniana* 'Lanei'
10 *Thuja occidentalis* 'Sunkist'
11 *Erica vagans* 'Mrs D F Maxwell'
12 *Tsuga canadensis* 'Pendula'
13 *Thymus drucei* 'Annie Hall'

Red Berries on Trees

Glowing red fruits create a stunningly attractive feature during autumn and often into winter, when they provide a further colour dimension in this often bleak season.

Ailanthus altissima

Tree of Heaven

Height: 7.5-10.5m (25-35ft)
Female trees bear conspicuous key-like reddish fruits.

Cotoneaster 'Cornubia'

Height: 4.5-6m (15-20ft)
A semi-evergreen tree with profuse crops of large red berries that often weigh down the branches.

Malus 'Red Sentinel'

Height: 3-4.5m (10-15ft)
The branches arch slightly with large crops of cardinal-red fruits that persist through to early spring

Sorbus aucuparia 'Asp:enifolia'

Rowan, Mountain Ash

Height: 4.5-7.5m (15-25ft)
A beautiful tree with deeply-cut fern-like leaves that turn red in autumn, matching its scarlet berries

CHAPTER ONE

THE FLOWER BORDER

It is spring when red and pink hardy herbaceous perennials really burst upon us, continuing to flower through to late summer and autumn. Two of the best late-flowering pink and red border flowers are *Anemone x hybrida* 'September Charm' and 'Queen Elizabeth'. When planted in a dominant clump they create a massed picture of colour. Unfortunately, in windy and exposed positions they can soon be battered by winds, but if given the protection of a low wall or surrounding shrubs they often survive with no ill-effect. They even thrive amid the shade of trees. Planted near an early autumn-colouring cherry tree such as *Prunus sargentii*, whose leaves assume orange and crimson tints, they look stunningly attractive. However, as with all garden planning, the vagaries of the weather can spoil this combination. More reliable plantings, timed to produce a foil for the clear pink single flowers of *Prunus sargentii* — as well as for many other pink-flowering prunus trees — are an underplanting of spring bulbs, such as *Chionodoxa sardensis* with its nodding sky-blue spring flowers.

The rhubarb family contains many beautiful ornamental plants for the flower garden. The edible species is *Rheum rhaponticum*, but there are others that will create attention as specimens in a hardy herbaceous border. *Rheum palmatum* 'Rubrum', which reaches 1.5m (5ft) high, develops large, deeply-cut purple-red leaves that change slowly to green after the 60-90cm (2-3ft) deep pinkish-red bead-like flowers fade towards the end of summer. It is best planted in groups of three or five plants, each 90cm (3ft) apart towards the back of a border.

The Californian Fuchsia, *Zauschneria californica*, is a border plant often claimed by both shrub and hardy herbaceous perennial enthusiasts. Botanically it is a 'half-hardy sub-shrubby perennial', but whatever its scientific classification it is an outstandingly attractive plant with its downy grey-green stems and leaves and terminal heads of 2.5-3cm (1-1¼in) long bright red and scarlet flowers which appear from late summer to autumn. It is best planted in a mixed or herbaceous border, where it gains protection from other plants.

Left: **Summer-bedding schemes** *need to create a mixture of colours, heights and textures, yet also be symmetrical and attractive.*

Acanthus mollis

Common Bear's Breeches (UK)
Artist's Acanthus (USA)

Acanthus plants are easily recognizable by their long, upright spires of tubular, rather foxglove-live flowers and handsome leaves. The most commonly grown species is *Acanthus mollis*, with white and purple flowers borne during mid to late summer in 45cm (1½ft) long spires. Others include *Acanthus spinosus*, the Spiny Bear's Breeches, and *Acanthus longifolius*, the Long-leaved Acanthus. Other common names, generally given to the whole group, are Bear's Breech and Bear's Foot.

Height: 90cm (3ft)
Spread: 75cm (2½ft)
Cultivation: Deeply cultivated well-drained soil and a sunny position suit this plant. It can be left to form large clumps; in autumn, cut these down to soil-level.
Propagation: Although seeds can be sown in spring in loam-based compost in pots placed in a cold frame, it is easier for the home gardener to propagate by lifting and dividing congested lumps in spring.

Left: **Acanthus mollis**
This dramatic herbaceous perennial displays purple and white flowers in long spires from mid to late summer. In small gardens just one plant is often enough, as the roots can be invasive.

Achillea millefolium

Yarrow (UK)
Common Yarrow · Milfoil ·
Sanguinary · Thousand Seal · Nose
Bleed (USA)

This is a well-known hardy creeping herbaceous perennial; the original wild species is often seen as a weed in lawns, pastures, meadows and grassy banks. Several attractive forms are now available and will enhance any mixed or herbaceous border. The deep green leaves provide a

Acanthus plants have had a marked influence on architecture. The leaves of *Acanthus spinosus*, Spiny Bear's Breeches, are said to have been the model for decorations in the Corinthian style of architecture.

perfect foil for the 10cm (4in) wide flattened flower heads from mid to late summer. The form 'Cerise Queen' displays cherry-red flowers, and 'Kelway' clear red heads.

Height: 60-75cm (2-2½ft)
Spread: 45cm (1½ft)
Cultivation: Any well-drained garden soil and a position in full sun suits this tolerant plant. In autumn cut down the stems to soil-level. Supporting the plants with twiggy sticks is necessary only in exposed areas. Remember to stake the plants early so that they grow up and through the supports.
Propagation: The easiest way to increase this plant is by lifting and dividing established plants in early spring.

Below: **Achillea millefolium 'Cerise Queen'** *This beautiful cherry-red form of the common Yarrow brings both colour and feathery deep green foliage to a mixed or herbaceous border.*

Alcea rosea

(Althaea rosea, Althaea chinensis)
Hollyhock (UK and USA)

This well-known hardy perennial is grown as an annual or biennial. Its funnel-shaped single or double pink flowers, to 10cm (4in) wide, are borne on short stalks from mid to late summer and even into early autumn. The light-green leaves have hairy surfaces.
Height: 2.1-2.7m (7-9ft) treated as a biennial; 1.3m (4½ft) treated as an annual.
Spread: 60cm (2ft)
Cultivation: Hollyhocks like fertile, relatively heavy, moisture-retentive soil and a sheltered position. They usually require staking when grown as biennials. They can be encouraged to flower for several years as perennials by cutting the stems down to within 15-20cm (6-8in) of soil-level after the flowers have faded. Hollyhocks treated in this way should be mulched with well-rotted manure or compost during the following spring and early summer. In exceptionally cold areas, cover the plants with cloches.
Propagation: To grow as an annual, sow seeds in late winter 6mm (¼in) deep in loam-based compost and keep at 10°C (50°F). When the seedlings are large enough to handle prick them off into pots and leave them in a cold frame to harden off. Plant out into the garden when all risk of frost has passed. To grow as a biennial, sow seeds 12mm (½in) deep in drills in the open garden in mid-summer. When the seedlings are large enough to handle — usually in late summer or early autumn — thin them out or transplant the young plants to 45-60cm (1½-2ft) apart. During spring of the following year set them in the garden. Remember that these plants will need staking. The supports should be unobtrusive.

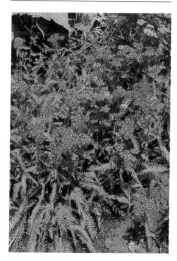

Right: **Alcea rosea**
This showy plant, often better known as Althaea rosea, can be grown as an annual or a biennial. It looks especially effective when planted against a wall, and is splendid for bringing late colour to a garden. It grows higher when cultivated as a biennial.

Achillea millefolium is a delightful plant for the flower border with a medicinal past. Old English herbalists called it Nose-bleed because its leaves promoted bleeding when applied to the nose.

Alcea rosea, with its large flowers on long spires, blends with many autumn-flowered plants. When grown as an annual or biennial rather than as a perennial, it is less susceptible to rust disease.

THE FLOWER BORDER

Amaryllis belladonna

(Hippeastrum equestre)
Belladonna Lily (UK)
Belladonna Lily · Cape Belladonna
Naked-lady Lily (USA)

A bulbous, somewhat tender plant with mid-green strap-like leaves from late winter to mid-summer. In late summer, these die down and the fragrant trumpet-shaped satiny pale-pink 10-13cm (4-5in) wide flowers appear on bare stems, usually in clusters of three or four, sometimes up to twelve.
Height: 60-75cm (2-2½ft)
Spread: 30-38cm (12-15in)
Cultivation:. Well-drained soil in a sunny and sheltered position is best. A site at the base of a south or west-facing wall is ideal. Late frosts will damage the early foliage. Set the bulbs in the soil in early summer, with 15-20cm (6-8in) of soil covering them. Remove dead flowers as they fade; also the leaves and stems when they die down.
Propagation: Clumps that become too large can be lifted in summer as soon as the leaves turn yellow. Divide and replant immediately.

Alstroemeria aurantiaca

Peruvian Lily (UK)
Peruvian Lily · Lily of the Incas (USA)

A richly-coloured, fleshy, tuberous-rooted Chilean herbaceous perennial, the hardiest of all alstroemerias. The trumpet-shaped 4-5cm (1½-2in) wide flowers, borne from mid to late summer, boast a range of colours, from rich orange to orange-scarlet. The long, lance-shaped leaves are glaucous (blue-grey) beneath.
Height: 90cm (3ft)
Spread: 38-45cm (15-18in)
Cultivation: Alstroemerias prefer fertile, well-drained, light soil and a sunny or partially shaded position. Set new plants (preferably pot-grown) in position during spring, 10-15cm (4-6in) deep. To encourage the development of

Above: **Alstroemeria aurantiaca**
This richly-coloured tuberous-rooted herbaceous perennial is ideal for mixed borders, where it creates colour during mid to late summer. The flowers are ideal for cutting for home decoration, when they last a long time in water.

further flowers, remove the blossoms as they fade, and in autumn cut the plants down to soil-level.
Propagation: New plants can be raised from seed sown in loam-based compost in spring and placed in a cold frame, but it is easier for the home gardener to lift and divide congested clumps in spring. Take care not to damage the roots. To produce a large number of plants lift and divide established clumps in mid-spring and pot up small individual pieces. Place in a cold frame.

Alstroemeria aurantiaca, with its vivid colours, needs a strong contrast from a large, spectacularly coloured shrub, such as the purple-leaved *Cotinus coggygria* 'Royal Purple'.

Amaryllis belladonna gained its common name Belladonna Lily in Italy from the fancied resemblance of its blend of red and white flowers to the complexion of a beautiful woman (*bella donna*).

Aster novi-belgii

Michaelmas Daisy (UK)
New England Aster (USA)

A beautiful and well-known herbaceous perennial. The original type came from North America and when introduced into Britain gained its common name because it flowers on Michaelmas (29 September), a significant feast day in the agricultural calendar. The plant has deep green, stem-clasping, slender-pointed leaves, and 5cm (2in) wide flowers borne in dense clusters during late summer and early autumn. Many pink and red forms are available, including 'Carnival' (semi-double, cherry-red), 'Freda Ballard' (semi-double, red), 'Patricia Ballard' (semi-double, pink), 'Raspberry Ripple' (double, carmine-red), 'Winston S. Churchill' (double,

glowing ruby-red), 'Orlando' (semi-double, pink), 'Fellowship' (semi-double, pink) and 'The Cardinal' (single, deep rose-red). There is also a range of dwarf forms, 30-45cm (1-1½ft) high.

Height: 90cm-1.2m (3-4ft)
Spread: 45-60cm (1½-2ft)
Cultivation: Fertile, well-drained but moisture-retentive soil (especially in late summer) is essential, as is a position in full sun. Most of the tall varieties will need staking with twiggy sticks. Do this early so that the plants grow up through the sticks and eventually hide them. After flowering, cut the plants down to soil level. The clumps are best divided every three years to prevent the quality of the flowers from deteriorating. Replant only young parts from around the edges of the clumps as these are young

and healthy; discard the old central portions.

Propagation: This is easily done by lifting and dividing clumps in early spring, every three years. To produce large numbers of plants *Aster novi-belgii* is best increased by lifting and dividing healthy clumps in mid-spring every spring and separating the healthy outside parts into small pieces. These can be planted in a nursery bed if very small or planted into the border. Because they are small they will have to be planted close together.

Below: **Aster novi-belgii 'Orlando'** *This richly coloured semi-double pink variety of Michaelmas Daisy brings life and colour to borders in late summer and into autumn. Fertile, well-drained but moisture-retentive soil is essential, and a sunny position.*

Below: **Amaryllis belladonna**
This exotic-looking bulbous border plant is useful for providing late summer colour. It does well among shrubs that provide some protection, or by a south or west-facing wall.

Aster novi-belgii and **Aster novae-angliae** are superb for late colour. They are ideal for mixed and herbaceous borders, while the dwarf forms of *Aster novi-belgii* are ideal for small town gardens.

THE FLOWER BORDER

Right: **Canna x generalis**
'Assault' *When planted in a group
in a summer-bedding scheme,
cannas are ideal for bringing
height and colour to the picture.
The flower heads appear
throughout summer.*

Canna x generalis

(Canna x hybrida)
Indian Shot (UK)
Common Garden Canna (USA)

An erect, large-leaved rhizomatous
hybrid, frequently used in summer-
bedding schemes. The leaves
reach 60cm (2ft) long and 30cm
(1ft) wide. There are two main
types of canna: those with purple
or brown leaves and those with
green ones. The 5-7.5cm (2-3in)
gladioli-like flowers are borne at
the tops of the stems during
summer. Outstanding forms
include 'Assault' (green leaves, red
flowers), 'Bonfire' (green leaves,
orange-scarlet flowers) and
'President' (green leaves, vivid
scarlet flowers).
Height: 90cm-1m (3-3½ft)
Spread: 38-45cm (15-18in)
Cultivation: During early spring,
plant the rhizomes in trays or large
pots of rich loam-based compost
and keep at 16°C (61°F). Before
planting them, give the rhizomes a
thorough soaking with water. They
will soon send up shoots; if more
than one shoot appears, split them
up and pot them. When they are
well established, pot them up into
a rich compost, and subsequently
into containers or beds where they
are to flower. Make sure you do
not do this until all risk of frost has
passed. In autumn, dig up the
plants or move them into a
greenhouse before the onset of
frosts.
Propagation: Divide the rhizomes
in early spring. Cannas can also be
increased from seed, although the
progeny will not resemble the
parents. Also, the seeds have
tough coats and require nicking
with a knife or soaking in water for
a day or so. Sow in late winter in a
high temperature.

Celosia argentea plumosa

(Celosia argentea pyramidalis)
*Prince of Wales' Feathers ·
Feathered Cockscomb (UK)*
*Cockcomb · Feathered Amaranth
(USA)*

A distinctive half-hardy annual
frequently grown as a houseplant
but also useful for summer-bedding
displays in mild areas outdoors.
Striking, feathery, 7.5-15cm (3-6in)
high flower plumes appear during
late summer in a range of colours.
Good forms include 'Apricot
Brandy' (orange-red), while others
have mixed colours — red, pink,
yellow and orange — as in
'Pampas Plume Mixed'.

Height: 38-60cm (15-24in)
Spread: 25-30cm (10-12in)
Cultivation: Fertile well-drained
soil and a sunny and sheltered
position are essential when
growing these plants outdoors. It is
not worth trying to grow them
outdoors in cold areas, as sudden
low-temperature spells soon check
their growth.
Propagation: During mid-spring,
sow seeds 3mm (⅛in) deep in
loam-based compost kept at 20°C
(68°F). When they are large
enough to handle, prick off the
seedlings into boxes or small pots
and slowly harden them off,
without sudden drops in
temperature. Plant them out into
the garden when all risk of frost
has passed.

Cannas, with their dark foliage, can be used to create
an interesting summer-bedding scheme with an
edging of light blue lobelias and a carpet of scarlet-
flowered *Begonia semperflorens* 'Indian Maid'.

Crocosmia masonorum

Montbretia (UK and USA)

A hardy corm-producing border plant with strap-like leaves, patterned pleats and ribs. The flame-orange flowers are borne from mid to late summer at the tips of the arching stems. A similar though less hardy plant is *Crocosmia x crocosmiiflora* (*Montbretia crocosmiiflora*). These are beautiful plants with 4cm (1½in) long trumpet-shaped flowers from mid to late summer. There are many exciting varieties, such as 'Bressingham Blaze' (orange-red), 'Emberglow' (orange-red) and 'Vulcan' (orange-red).

Height: 75cm (2½ft)

Spread: 20-25cm (8-10in)

Cultivation: Light, well-drained and fertile soil is best, but do not let the soil dry out during summer. Crocosmias appreciate a sunny position. Set the corms in position in early spring, 5-7.5cm (2-3in) deep and 15cm (6in) apart. In warm areas the plants can be left in the soil to form large clumps, but in exceptionally cold areas lift the plants in late autumn, dry off the corms and store them over winter. When storing the corms keep them neither too dry, or they will shrivel, nor too damp, or they will rot.

Propagation: Large clumps left in the soil can be lifted and divided just after flowering, or you can wait until spring.

Above: **Crocosmia masonorum**
This spectacular plant for summer colour is hardier than others of its genus. The flowers can be cut for house decoration. In mild areas it can be left in the ground to form large clumps.

Left: **Celosia argentea plumosa 'Apricot Brandy'** *This distinctive half-hardy annual needs a warm and sheltered position. The plume-like flowers last for many weeks in summer and contrast well with the light green foliage.*

Celosia argentea plumosa is often used in formal bedding schemes, but it can also look effective planted as a filler in mixed borders or with hardy annuals. Take care not to overwater plants.

Crocosmia x crocosmiiflora forms a stately display in mixed borders. Several varieties are available, including 'Bressingham Blaze' (orange-red flowers), 'Emberglow' (orange-red) and 'Vulcan' (orange-red).

Left: **Cuphea miniata 'Firefly'**
This busy, highly branched hardy annual bears masses of bright scarlet flowers during summer. It is best planted in the centre of the annual border as it does not require staking.

Dahlia

These reliable and well-known garden flowers can be divided into two main groups: those that can be grown as half-hardy annuals for use in bedding schemes; and those that are best grown as perennials in mixed borders, mingling with herbaceous plants and flowering shrubs.

BEDDING DAHLIAS

These half-hardy perennials from Mexico are grown as half-hardy annuals, displaying 5-7.5cm (2-3in) wide single, double or semi-double flowers from mid-summer to autumn. There are many varieties in a wide colour range, in mixed and self-colours.

Height: 30-50cm (12-20in)
Spread: 38-45cm (15-24in)
Cultivation: Well-cultivated, fertile, compost or manure-enriched soil and a sunny position suits bedding dahlias. If the soil is too rich, however, the plants produce excessive foliage at the expense of flowers. There is no need to stake them – unlike the large border types. Removal of dead flowers encourages the plants to produce further blooms. Water the plants during dry spells.
Propagation: During late winter and early spring, sow seeds 6mm (¼in) deep in a loam-based seed compost at 16°C (61°F). When they are large enough to handle, prick off the seedlings into boxes or small pots of loam-based compost and slowly harden them off in a cold frame. Set them out in the garden as soon as all risk of frost has passed.

BORDER DAHLIAS

These are half-hardy tuberous plants, easily damaged by frost, that quickly bring colour to the garden. There are several

Cuphea miniata

A spectacular Mexican half-hardy perennial grown as a half-hardy annual. Cupheas bear slender-pointed mid-green leaves covered with white bristles. During mid-summer and into autumn, they produce a fine display of bright-red 4cm (1½in) long tubular flowers. Often grown as a pot plant for a cool greenhouse or conservatory, they can also be used in summer-bedding schemes. The form 'Firefly' has brilliant scarlet flowers.
Height: 45-60cm (1½-2ft)
Spread: 38-45cm (15-18in)

Cultivation: Any ordinary garden soil suits cupheas, and they can be grown in full sun or light shade.
Propagation: During spring, sow seeds 6mm (¼in) deep in loam-based compost at 15°C (59°F). When they are large enough to handle, prick the seedlings off into loam-based compost and harden them off in a cold frame. After all risk of frost is over, set the plants out in the garden. Alternatively, the seedlings can be pricked off into small pots of loam-based compost, and potted up into larger pots as the plants grow. When they have become sizeable plants they can be taken indoors.

Cuphea also does well as a pot plant for the home or greenhouse. Sow seeds in spring and prick out the seedlings into small pots of loam-based compost. Pot up into larger pots when the roots become pot-bound.

classifications and many varieties.

Anemone-flowered
(60cm-1m/2-3½ft): These have
double flowers with flat outer
petals and short, tubular inner
ones. Flowering is from mid-
summer to the frosts of autumn.

Ball-type (90cm-1.2m/3-4ft): As the
name implies, these have ball-
shaped flowers, with tubular, blunt-
ended petals. There are *Small Ball*
types with blooms 10-15cm (4-6in)
wide, and *Miniature Ball* forms with
flowers up to 10cm (4in) wide.

Cactus and Semi-cactus
(90cm-1.5m/3-5ft): These are sub-
divided into five groups, *Miniature*
(blooms up to 10cm/4in wide);
Small (blooms 10-15cm/4-6in wide);
Medium (blooms 15-20cm/6-8in);
Large (blooms 20-25cm/8-10in
wide); and *Giant* (blooms
25cm/10in or more wide). Cactus
types have petals rolled back or
quilled for more than half their
length. Semi-cactus types have
similar petals, but quilled or rolled
back for less than half their length.

Collarettes (75cm-1.2m/2½-4ft):
These have blooms with a single
outer ring of flat ray florets, with a
ring of small florets in the centre,
forming a disc.

Decoratives: These have double
flowers without central discs. They
are formed of broad, flat ray
florets. This group is further divided
into: *Miniature* (90cm-1.2m/3-4ft):
These have flowers up to 10cm
(4in) wide. *Small* (1-1.2m/3½-4ft):
Flowers 10-15cm (4-6in) wide.
Medium (1-1.2m/3½-4ft): Flowers
15-20cm (6-8in) wide. *Large*
(1-1.5m/3½-5ft): Flowers 20-25cm
(8-10in) wide. *Giant* (1.2-1.5m/4-5ft):
Flowers 25cm (10in) or more wide.

Paeony-flowered (up to 90cm/3ft):
The flowers are formed of two or
more rings of flat ray flowers, with
a central disc.

Pompon (90cm-1.2m/3-4ft): The
flowers closely resemble those of
Ball types, but are more globular
and are no more than 5cm (2in)
wide. The florets curl inwards for
their entire length.

Single-flowered
(45-75cm/1½-2½ft): These display

flowers up to 10cm (4in) wide, with
a single row of petals arranged
around a central disc.

Cultivation: Well-drained soil, with
plenty of moisture-retentive
compost or well-decomposed
manure added, is required. Include
a sprinkling of bonemeal before
setting the tubers in the ground
during mid to late spring at 10cm
(4in) deep. If sprouted tubers are
used, take care that they are not
planted too early, or frost will
damage them. The young plants
will need staking for support.
Nip out the growing tips of all
shoots to encourage sideshoots to
develop, and if you want large
flowers, remove sideshoots and
buds from around the developing
flowers. The removal of dead
flowers helps the development of
further flowers.

Above: **Dahlia 'Bishop of
Llandaff'**
*This is a paeony-flowered type with
rings of flat crimson petals
surrounding a central core of
stamens. Its foliage is dark and
although it is a dahlia used in
bedding schemes, at 75cm (2½ft)
high it grows taller than most
varieties used for bedding.*

In autumn, carefully dig up the
tubers about a week after the
foliage has been blackened by
frost. Remove soil from the tubers
and store them upside down for a
few weeks to encourage them to
dry out. Then place them in boxes
of peat in a dry, frost-proof position
until the following year.

Propagation: The easiest way for
the home gardener to do this is to
divide the tubers in spring.

Formal planting schemes for bedding dahlias are
easy to create. One example is as a carpet of
salmon-pink and cherry-red dot plants, with an edging
of pale blue lobelia.

Ball types to look for include 'Alltami Cherry' (small
ball, vivid scarlet), 'Biddenham Serene' (small ball,
dark crimson), 'Direct Hit' (miniature ball, scarlet) and
'Valerie Buller' (miniature, plum red).

THE FLOWER BORDER

Above: **Dahlia 'Alva's Doris'**
*A beautiful bright crimson small
cactus dahlia, 10-15cm (4-6in)
wide. It rises to 1-1.2m (3½-4ft)
high with a spread of 75cm (2½ft
wide. It is dominantly coloured.*

Left: **Dahlia 'Geerling's Elite'**
*A brilliantly-coloured free-flowering
collarette variety, this has orient-
red petals tipped buff, and a buff
collar. It rises to 1m (3½ft) and is
ideal for setting towards the front
of a mixed border.*

Decorative types to look for include 'Hamari Girl'
(giant dec., pink), 'Jo's Choice' (miniature dec., red),
'Festive Season' (small dec., yellow and red) and
'Liberator' (giant dec., rich crimson scarlet).

Top right: **Dahlia 'Scarlet Comet'**
*An anemone-flowered variety with
brilliantly-coloured flowers formed
of an inner ring of petals that
surround the centre like a halo. It
is ideal for bringing an intense
splash of colour to a border.*

Right: **Dahlia 'Salmon Keene'**
*This cactus-type displays the rolled
or 'quilled' petals distinctive of this
group. It produces attractively
spiked flowers that will enhance a
border.*

Cactus types to look for include 'Athalie' (semi-
cactus, pink blends), 'Elmbrook Rebel' (giant semi-
cactus, deep red),'Doc Van Horn' (large semi-cactus,
pink) and 'Alva's Doris (small cactus, blood red).

Euphorbia griffithii 'Fireglow'

Spurge (UK)

An attractive perennial with lance-shaped, mid-green leaves and orange-red bracts at the top of the stems during early summer.
Height: 60-75cm (2-2½ft)
Spread: 60-75cm (2-2½ft)
Cultivation: Fertile, well-drained soil and a position in full sun suit euphorbias. Set the plants in position in spring or early autumn.
Propagation: The plants are easily increased by lifting and dividing large clumps in spring or autumn.

Dicentra spectabilis

Bleeding Heart (UK and USA)

This widely-grown Chinese and Japanese herbaceous perennial has long been known as Bleeding Heart, but at the turn of the century it was the North American *Dicentra canadensis* that laid claim to this common name. *D. spectabilis* is often called Dutchman's Breeches, but this name is more accurately applied to *D. cucullaria*, another North American plant. At one time *D. spectabilis* was aptly called Chinaman's Breeches, which accurately related to the region from which the plant came. But whatever its common name, this plant is a most attractive addition to any garden. Its grey-green, finely-divided and rather fern-like leaves are a perfect foil for the 2.5cm (1in) long, pendulous, rose-red, heart-shaped flowers, borne on arching stems during early to mid-summer.
Height: 45-75cm (1½-2½ft)
Spread: 45cm (1½ft)
Cultivation: Rich, well-cultivated fertile soil and a sheltered, sunny or partially shaded position suit this plant. The roots are somewhat brittle, so the plants are best left undisturbed once established.
Propagation: It is easily increased by carefully lifting and dividing established clumps in spring or autumn.

Above: **Dicentra spectabilis**
This well-known and distinctive hardy herbaceous perennial with dainty flowers needs well-cultivated fertile soil in full sun or partial shade. The flowers appear from early to mid-summer.

Below: **Euphorbia griffithii 'Fireglow'** *This unusual perennial has red-tipped shoots that arise from the soil. In early summer the appearance of the foliage is enhanced by strikingly attractive, bright orange-red bracts.*

Dicentra cucullaria, or Dutchman's Breeches, is native to North America and was once commonly found wild in New York State. Its Dutch connection is that New York was once called New Amsterdam.

Left: **Freesia 'Red Star'**
Although normally grown in the greenhouse, a few varieties of freesia, such as this one, are suitable for growing outdoors. The flowers are brightly coloured and highly scented. Plant the corms in spring.

Freesia x kewensis

This well-known South African tender, corm-bearing plant produces the sweetly-scented 2.5-5cm (1-2in) long fragrant blooms so often sold as cut flowers for home decoration. These hybrids, often known as *Freesia x hybrida*, have narrow mid-green leaves and, when planted outside in spring, produce flowers during late summer. They are not hardy enough to be left outside all year. Many forms are available, in a wide colour range. Red and pink varieties include 'Red Star' (red), 'Rose Marie' (rose-pink), 'Madame Curie' (red) and 'Nieuw Amsterdam' (magenta).

Height: 45-60cm (1½-2ft)
Spread: 13-20cm (5-8in)
Cultivation: Fertile, light, sandy soil and a sheltered sunny position suit freesias. During spring, plant the corms about 5cm (2in) deep. Use small twiggy sticks to support the foliage, and in autumn, when the foliage has turned yellow, lift the plants and corms. Dry off the corms and remove the offsets. In mild areas and in well-drained light and sandy soils it is possible to leave the corms outside all winter. Corms planted in late summer to early autumn will flower in late spring. Although freesias can be induced to flower in a greenhouse, a temperature of 5°C (45°F) is needed. Plant the corms in boxes or pots of loam-based compost in late summer and early autumn to bring about flowering from mid-winter to spring. Ensure you maintain the right temperature.
Propagation: Although seeds can be sown in late winter and spring, it is easier for home gardeners to remove the corms and offsets and to replant these in spring.

Euphorbia griffithii provides a screen of leaves from soil level to the orange-red bracts at the tops of shoots. Its clear outline allows it to be positioned just 30cm (1ft) in from the edge of a border.

THE FLOWER BORDER

Above: **Galega officinalis**
These plants have a sprawling habit, but create a superb colour patch, with their small pea-shaped flowers borne on branching stems with attractive, narrow leaves.

Galega officinalis

Goat's Rue (UK and USA)

A bushy and sprawling hardy herbaceous perennial with light green, short-stalked, compound leaves formed of many leaflets and best seen at the back of a border. During mid-summer it produces dense clusters of pale lilac or white flowers in short spires. The form 'Her Majesty' is well-known for its soft lilac-blue flowers.
Height: 1-1.5m (3½-5ft)
Spread: 75cm (2½ft)
Cultivation: Any well-drained garden soil and a position in full sun or light shade are suitable. Ideally, position it for a dominant display, with a grouping of three or five plants at the back of the border. After flowering, cut the stems down to soil-level.
Propagation: Although it can be increased by sowing seeds in spring in a nursery bed, it is much easier to increase by lifting and dividing large clumps in spring or autumn.

Galega officinalis best displays its charms at the back of a border. The lilac-blue forms look best set against a high old brick wall, whereas the white form is superb with a backcloth of clear sky.

Large-flowered gladioli are ideal for setting in mixed borders, where they create bright colour while shrubs and border plants are becoming established. Set them in groups of one colour rather than a mixture.

Gladiolus: Large-flowered Hybrids

Sword Lily (UK)
Corn Flag · Sword Lily (USA)

These are the well-known, large-flowered, corm-bearing plants that create such spectacular displays from mid to late summer. The erect spikes of flowers are often 50cm (20in) long, formed of florets 10-18cm (4-7in) wide in a wide colour range, with many lovely reds and pinks. These include 'Aristocrat' (velvety garnet-red), 'Dr Fleming' (light salmon-pink with cream throats), 'Jo Wagenaar' (blood-scarlet, with a velvety sheen), 'Life Flame' (vivid red), 'Ardent' (cherry-red), 'Flos Florium' (salmon-pink), 'Memorial Day' (reddish-magenta) and 'President de Gaulle' (orange-red).
Height: 75cm-1m (2½-3½ft)
Spread: 20-25cm (8-10in)
Cultivation: Ordinary well-drained garden soil and a position in full sun assure success for this reliable favourite. Plant the corms in mid-spring, 10cm (4in) deep in heavy soil but 15cm (6in) in light soils. Anchored at these depths, the plants will not require staking in sheltered areas. In exposed positions, support the stems with small canes. After flowering, when the foliage turns yellow, carefully dig up the plants and allow them to dry for a week or so. Cut off the stems 12mm (½in) above the corms if they have not already broken off, and remove all soil. Then store them in shallow boxes in a cool and vermin-proof position. It should also be dry.
Propagation: In autumn, when the corms are lifted and dried for storage, remove the cormlets from around them. During spring, plant these in drills 5cm (2in) deep in a nursery bed.

Above: **Godetia grandiflora 'Dwarf Vivid'** *This beautiful hardy annual grows well in most soils. Avoid excessively rich ones that encourage leaf growth at the expense of flowers.*

Godetia grandiflora

(Godetia whitneyi)

This beautiful, compact. hardy annual from western North America has light green, lance-shaped leaves that present a superb foil for the 5cm (2in) wide rose-purple, funnel-shaped flowers during mid-summer and into late summer. Many single and double varieties are now available, in a wide colour range. These include 'Dwarf Vivid' (dark pink), 'Crimson Glow' (crimson) and 'Sybil Sherwood' (salmon-pink).
Height: 30-38cm (12-15in)
Spread: 20-25cm (8-10in)
Cultivation: Light and moist soil and a position in full sun suit it best. Avoid excessively rich soils that encourage lush foliage at the expense of flowers.
Propagation: In late spring, sow seeds 6mm (¼in) deep where they are to flower. When they are large enough to handle, thin out the seedlings to 15cm (6in) apart.

Above: **Godetia grandiflora 'Sybil Sherwood'** *This is a beautiful hardy annual that produces a mass of single salmon-pink and white flowers from mid to late summer. It creates delicately-coloured mounds.*

Left: **Gladiolus 'Aristocrat'**
This is a beautiful large-flowered gladiolus that gives a reliable garden display. The colour range is wide and includes many red and pink shades.

Godetia grandiflora can also be grown as a houseplant. Sow seeds thinly in pots or boxes of loam-based compost in late summer. Pot up the seedlings and grow them on in a cool greenhouse.

THE FLOWER BORDER

Hemerocallis 'Pink Damask'

Day Lily (UK and USA)

A superb hardy herbaceous perennial with stiff, arching, bright green sword-like leaves and lily-like flowers, 13-21cm (5-7in) wide. This form develops warm pink flowers with yellow throats during mid to late summer. Other pink and red forms include 'Holiday Mood' (bright red), 'Hornby Castle' (deep brick red with a yellow throat), 'Morocco Red' (dusky red with a yellow cup), 'Stafford' (deep red with an orange throat) and 'Pink Prelude' (pink).

Height: 75-90cm (2½-3ft)
Spread: 45-60cm (1½-2ft)
Cultivation: Good garden soil that does not dry out during summer and a position in full sun or light shade are best for Day Lilies. Once planted, they can be left in the same position for many years. In autumn cut the plants down to soil-level.
Propagation: Day Lilies are easily increased by lifting and dividing overcrowded clumps in spring or autumn. Replant the divided roots immediately.

Heuchera sanguinea

Coral Flower · Coral Bells (UK)
Coral Bells (USA)

This bright and cheerful hardy perennial from Mexico and Arizona has attractive, evergreen, round or heart-shaped, dark green leaves. The small, bell-shaped, bright red flowers are borne in lax heads on long and wiry stems from mid-summer to autumn. Several superb forms are available, including 'Firebird' (intense deep red), 'Red Spangles' (crimson-scarlet), 'Scintillation' (pink, tipped red),

Left: **Heuchera sanguinea 'Red Spangles'**
This is a beautiful Coral Flower with crimson-scarlet flowers borne on slender stems from mid-summer to autumn. Light soil is needed: do not plant in a clay soil.

Hemerocallis are admirable for setting in a mixed or herbaceous border, to which they contribute both height and colour. Also, their stiff, upright form means they look good alongside paths.

Heuchera sanguinea is a delight at the edge of a border and can be blended with yellow roses, such as Rosa 'Buff Beauty'. It also looks good mixed with the magenta-flowered *Geranium psilostemon*.

Kniphofia

Red Hot Poker · Torch Lily · Flame Flower (UK)
Torch Lily · Poker Plant · Red Hot Poker · Tritoma (USA)

These well-known hardy herbaceous perennials produce distinctive poker-like heads from mid-summer to autumn. There are many hybrids, as well as true species, in a height range from 45cm-1.5m (1½-5ft). In colour they range from yellow and orange to red, and include 'Samuel's Scarlet' (height 1.5m/5ft, flowers bright scarlet-red), *Kniphofia uvaria* (90cm/3ft, red orange and yellow), *Kniphofia macowanii* (75cm/2½ft, deep orange-red), *Kniphofia nelsonii* 'Major' (75cm/2½ft, flame-red), *Kniphofia rufa* (60cm/2ft, yellow tipped red), *Kniphofia praecox* (1.5-1.8m/5-6ft, brilliant scarlet).

Cultivation: Kniphofias like well-drained, fertile soil in full sun. It is essential that the soil does not remain wet during winter. Give the plants a mulch of well-rotted manure or compost in spring.

Propagation: The easiest way to increase the plants is by lifting and dividing large clumps in late spring. True species breed true from seeds, which can be sown 12mm (½in) deep in seedbeds in spring.

'Splendour' (salmon-scarlet) and 'Sunset' (bright red).

Height: 30-45cm (1-1½ft)

Spread: 38-45cm (15-18in)

Cultivation: Well-drained relatively light soil in full sun or light shade suits heucheras best. Set new plants in the soil in spring or autumn. After flowering, cut down the stems.

Propagation: Heucheras are easily increased by lifting and dividing old plants in spring. This usually needs to be done every three or four years, particularly when the crowns appear to rise out of the ground. Heucheras can also be raised by sowing seeds in early spring boxes of loam-based compost placed in a cold frame. When large enough to handle, plant out seedlings into a nursery bed. Plants will be ready for the garden in autumn.

Above: **Hemerocallis 'Pink Damask'**
An eye-catching Day Lily, this variety boasts warm pink flowers with yellow throats. It is ideal for planting and leaving in one position for a long time. The flowers last for only a day, but are quickly replenished by further flowers that create colour over a period of several months in summer.

Right: **Kniphofia praecox**
This beautiful tall herbaceous perennial has stiff stems bearing torch-like brilliant scarlet flowers in late summer and into early autumn. They look best when planted in a dominant display with the bright torch-like heads silhouetted against blue sky, and are ideal for use in island beds where the plants are grown without supports.

Kniphofias are superb in a bed of their own, using just one species or variety. They are at their best when filling a bed that slopes down to water, but also look good in large gaps left between paving slabs.

THE FLOWER BORDER

Lilium 'Enchantment'

This distinctive and widely-grown hardy Asiatic stem-rooting lily, bears heads of up to sixteen cup-shaped, nasturtium-red flowers up to 15cm (6in) wide in mid-summer. Another superb lily from the same group is 'Cover Girl', with stunningly attractive, demure-pink flowers.

Height: 90cm-1.2m (3-4ft)
Spread: 20-30cm (8-12in)
Cultivation: Fertile, well-drained soil in full sun or light shade assures success. Set the bulbs in position, 10-15cm (4-6in) deep, from late autumn to early spring. Although it must be well-drained, the soil should also retain moisture, so during spring and summer keep the surface well mulched with peat or compost. Ensure the soil is moist before adding this moisture-retentive material. In sheltered gardens the lilies do not need staking, but on windswept sites — which really should be avoided — support from thin bamboo canes may be necessary.
Propagation: Every three or four years, lift and divide the congested clumps during late autumn or early spring.

Lavatera trimestris

(Lavatera rosea)
Mallow (UK)

This is one of the most beautiful of all hardy annuals, with a bushy habit and pale green, smooth, roughly heart-shaped, lobed leaves. The 10cm (4in) wide, glowing pink flowers are borne profusely from mid to late summer from the leaf-joints of the top leaves. Several forms are available, including 'Silver Cup' (silver-pink) and 'Sutton's Loveliness' (rose-pink).
Height: 60-90cm (2-3ft)
Spread: 45-50cm (18-20in)
Cultivation: Moderately rich garden soil and a sheltered but sunny site are best for mallows.
Propagation: During mid and late spring, sow seeds where the plants are to flower, setting them 12mm (½in) deep. When the seedlings are large enough to handle, thin them to 50-60cm (20-24in) apart.

Above: **Lavatera trimestris** *'Silver Cup' This beautiful hardy annual is a gem in any garden, and is also ideal as a cut flower for home decoration. Avoid sowing the seeds in very rich soil, which encourages lush leaf growth at the expense of flowers.*

Below: **Lavatera trimestris** *A superb setting for this hardy annual is to contrast it with the woolly grey-leaved hardy shrub Ballota pseudodictamnus.*

Lavetera trimestris, like many delicate pink flowers, needs careful positioning if it is not to be dominated by other colours. Mix it with grey foliage plants, such as the low shrub *Ballota pseudodictamnus*.

Lilium 'Enchantment' is ideal among rhododendrons and azaleas beneath a light canopy of tall pines. Lilies are useful for extending colour in a group of azaleas, which often look bleak in mid-season.

Linum grandiflorum 'Rubrum'

Scarlet Flax (UK)
Flowering Flax (USA)

This hardy annual with 4cm (1½in) wide, single, saucer-shaped scarlet flowers comes from Algeria. The flowers are borne from mid to late summer on wispy stems above a mat of narrow, pale green, pointed leaves. So wispy are the stems, even the slightest breeze sets them moving.

Height: 38-45cm (15-18in)
Spread: 20-25cm (8-10in)
Cultivation: Any good well-drained soil in full sun suits flaxes.
Propagation: During spring or early summer, sow seeds 6mm (¼in) deep where the plants are to flower. When they are large enough to handle, thin the seedlings to 13cm (5in) apart.

Below: **Linum grandiflorum 'Rubrum'** *This spectacular hardy annual has bright scarlet flowers from mid to late summer. A sunny position is essential for the rich colouring of the flowers.*

Below: **Lilium 'Enchantment'**
This really spectacular Asiatic lily, has clustered heads of cup-shaped flowers up to 15cm (6in) wide. It delights in a sunny position.

Above: **Lilium 'Cover Girl'**
An appealing Asiatic lily, this variety has large, wide open flowers that provide colour in a border in sun or light shade.

Lilies need moist soil and by setting them amid low, large-leaved plants, such as hostas, the ground will stay cool and damp. Variegated forms will supply colour when the lilies are not in flower.

Linum grandiflorum can also be grown as a pot plant for spring colour. Sow seeds thinly in late summer; thin to six seedlings per pot when large enough to handle and grow in a cold greenhouse.

THE FLOWER BORDER

Lobelia cardinalis

Cardinal Flower (UK)
Cardinal Flower · Indian Pink (USA)

A stunningly impressive though short-lived North American hardy herbaceous perennial with erect stems bearing oblong, lance-shaped, mid-green leaves and brilliant scarlet, 2.5cm (1in) wide, five-lobed flowers during mid to late summer.

Height: 75-90cm (2½-3ft)
Spread: 30-39cm (12-15in)
Cultivation: Rich, fertile, moist soil and a partially shaded position suit this plant. Fork in generous amounts of peat or well-rotted manure when preparing the soil. Set the plants in position in spring.
Propagation: In near-frost-free gardens the plants can be left in the soil throughout winter, but in all other areas dig up the roots in autumn and store them throughout winter in a cold frame or greenhouse. In spring, separate the rosettes and box them up in peaty soil until well established. They can then be planted in the garden.

Left: **Lobelia 'Cherry Ripe'**
This is one of the best known and spectacular of the many hybrids of Lobelia cardinalis *and* Lobelia fulgens, *producing brilliant scarlet flowers in late summer on stems up to 1.2m (4ft) high.*

Lychnis coronaria

(Agrostemma coronaria)
Crowned Campion (UK)
Rose Campion · Mullein Pink ·
Dusty Miller (USA)

This beautiful, short-lived perennial has silvery, woolly-textured, lance-shaped, leathery leaves and 12mm (½in) wide, rich crimson, rather bell-shaped flowers, borne in loose round heads from mid to late summer. The form 'Abbotswood Rose' boasts sprays of intense rose pink, while 'Atrosanguinea' has strong red flowers.
Height: 45-60cm (1½-2ft)
Spread: 30-38cm (12-15in)

Lobelias are named in honour of the Belgian botanist Matthias de Lobel (1538-1616). He went to England in 1584, and became physician to James I of England (James II of Scotland).

Lychnis coronaria is perfect for filling gaps in borders, where it blends well with many plants, including Rosemary (*Rosmarinus officinalis*), achilleas, Red Hot Pokers and African Lilies.

Cultivation: Any well-drained garden soil in full sun or light shade suits lychnis. In exposed areas it requires support from twiggy sticks, and removing dead flower-heads prevents the formation of seeds.

Propagation: Because it is only short-lived as a perennial, it is best grown as an annual. Sow seeds in late winter in loam-based compost at 13°C (55°F). When they are large enough to handle, prick out the seedlings into boxes of loam-based compost and slowly harden them off, eventually in a cold frame. Plant them out into the garden during late spring at 23-30cm (9-12in) apart. Alternatively, sow the seeds in mid-summer where the plants are to flower the following year. Thin the seedlings when they appear to 23-30cm (9-12in) apart.

Lythrum salicaria

Purple Loosestrife (UK)
Purple Loosestrife · Spiked Loosestrife (USA)

A beautiful resilient and reliable hardy herbaceous perennial with lance-shaped, mid-green leaves and handsome, reddish-purple flowers, borne in spires 23-30cm (9-12in) long during mid-summer and into early autumn. Several superb forms are available, including 'Firecandle' (intense rosy-red), 'Lady Sackville' (bright rose-pink), 'Robert' (clear pink) and 'The Beacon' (deep rose-crimson).
Height: 75cm-1.2m (2½-4ft)
Spread: 45cm (1½ft)
Cultivation: Moisture-retentive soil in a sunny position suits it best, although it does quite well in ordinary garden soil. After flowering cut back the stems to soil-level.
Propagation: The roots can be divided in spring or autumn, but often old clumps become very woody and difficult to divide. Instead, take cuttings 7.5cm (3in) long from the base of the plant during spring and insert them in pots placed in a cold frame.

Above: **Lychnis coronaria 'Abbotswood Rose'** *This short-lived perennial displays loose heads of intense rose-pink flowers from mid to late summer. The silvery foliage is an attractive bonus with this border brightener.*

Below: **Lythrum salicaria 'Firecandle'** *This popular herbaceous perennial displays intense rosy-red flowers from mid-summer to early autumn. It does not grow well in deep shade, preferring a sunny position.*

Lythrum salicaria does best when grown in moist soil, where it enjoys the company of polygonums, *Euphorbia palustris* with its sulphur-yellow flower heads, and a range of moisture-loving grasses.

Nerine bowdenii

This pretty South African bulbous plant from Cape Province is not totally hardy in extremely cold areas. It has narrow, strap-like, mid-green leaves which develop after the flowers appear from late summer to early winter. The distinctive rose or deep pink flowers are each formed of six strap-like petals usually twisted at their ends. They are borne in heads of up to eight flowers, at the end of stiff stems up to 60cm (2ft) long. The most popular form is 'Fenwick's Variety', with deep pink flowers.

Height: 50-60cm (20-24in)
Spread: 15-20cm (6-8in)
Cultivation: Any good well-drained soil and a sunny position against a south or west-facing wall are suitable. Once established, the plants can be left in position to produce a spectacular display. However, when they are too cramped and congested, the number of flower stems decreases.
Propagation: Every four or five years, lift and divide overcrowded clumps. The plant can also be increased by sowing the soft, fleshy seeds in loam-based compost during late spring.

Macleaya microcarpa

(Bocconia microcarpa)
Plume Poppy (UK)

A large, graceful, hardy herbaceous perennial from Northern China, somewhat resembling *Macleaya cordata*. However, *M. microcarpa* has feathery pink plumes with a bronze appearance that makes it quite distinctive and the flowers are produced a couple of weeks earlier, from mid to late summer. They are best positioned at the back of a border, where they can be given plenty of room. The plume-like heads flower above other plants and create a very attractive background. These plants spread rapidly by invasive underground suckers.

Height: 1.5-2.4m (5-8ft)
Spread: 90cm-1m (3-3½ft)
Cultivation: Rich, fertile relatively light soil suits the Plume Poppy. Give it a site sheltered enough to prevent its tall stems being blown and battered by strong wind. Twiggy sticks are needed to support the plants. In autumn, cut them down to soil-level.
Propagation: The invasive roots can be lifted and divided in spring or autumn, and for the home gardener this is the easiest method. Alternatively, 5-7.5cm (2-3in) long cuttings from basal shoots can be taken in early summer and inserted in pots containing equal parts of peat and sharp sand, placed in a cold frame. Pot up the plants when they are well rooted.

Above: **Macleaya microcarpa**
A beautiful herbaceous perennial with feathery plumes. It is an invasive plant and because of this it is not very well suited to small gardens.

Top right: **Nerine bowdenii**
An eye-catching bulbous plant for autumn flowers. It needs a warm, sunny and sheltered position, and the leaves appear after the flowers.

Right: **Paeonia officinalis 'Rubra Plena'** *A beautiful large-flowered herbaceous perennial, sometimes called the Old Double Crimson Paeony, with crimson-red flowers in early to mid-summer. Once established it is best to leave it alone, undisturbed.*

Macleaya microcarpa is ideal for filling a large corner position against a wall. Its tall flower plumes are ideal for breaking up the often imposing nature of a large brick wall.

Nerine bowdenii is best given a relatively narrow border against a warm wall all to itself. Its late flowering makes it a tricky plant to combine effectively with others.

Paeonia officinalis

Common Garden Paeony (UK)

A distinctive and well-known herbaceous perennial, more popular in the past than today, but still deserving a position in a mixed border, where it often appears more at home than in a traditional herbaceous border. The large, deeply incised mid-green leaves are a perfect foil for the 13cm (5in) wide, single crimson flowers that appear on stiff stems in early to mid-summer. This form, however, is rarely seen and it is the forms such as 'Rubra Plena' (crimson-red), 'Rosea Plena' (deep pink) and 'Alba Plena' (pink at first, fading to white) that are mainly grown. *Paeonia lactiflora*, also known as *P. albiflora*, is another herbaceous perennial and rises to about 60cm (2ft) high. The true type bears 7.5-10cm (3-4in) wide single, white and scented flowers in early summer. However, there are many forms in pink and red, which can be up to 18cm (7in) wide. These include the double and scented 'Albert Crousse' with bright pink flowers; 'Bower of Roses' with rose-crimson double blooms; 'Bowl of Beauty' displaying soft pink semi-double flowers with golden stamens; 'Globe of Light' with pale rose-pink blooms; 'Karl Rosenfeld' displaying wine-red double flowers; 'Lady Alexandra Duff' with soft pink double and scented flowers; the single blue-pink 'Pink Delight'; 'President Roosevelt' with deep red double flowers; and the well-known 'Sarah Bernhardt' with scented, double, pink flowers. These are dominantly-flowered plants and soon create interest in the garden.
Height: 75-90cm (2½-3ft)
Spread: 90cm (3ft)
Cultivation: Paeonies thrive in a rich, well-drained but moisture-retentive soil in full sun or light shade. When preparing the soil, dig in plenty of well-rotted manure or compost.
Propagation: During early spring or autumn, lift and divide large clumps.

Paeonia officinalis is originally a native of Southern Europe, from France to Albania. The true species is difficult to obtain, though there are several excellent hybrid varieties.

THE FLOWER BORDER

Papaver orientale

Oriental Poppy (UK and USA)

This hardy and stunningly attractive herbaceous perennial with rough, bristly, hairy stems and leaves is a wonderful scene-setter. The mid to deep green leaves are deeply incised, with the 9-10cm (3½-4in) wide scarlet flowers with black centres appearing during early to mid-summer. There are now many forms to choose from, including 'Enchantress' (carmine-pink), 'Allegro' (bright orange-scarlet), 'Goliath' (crimson-scarlet), 'Ladybird' (vermilion-red), 'Marcus Perry' (orange-scarlet), 'Turkish Delight' (flesh pink) and 'Cedric's Pink' (pink and curled petals with a purple-black blotch at the base).
Height: 60-90cm (2-3ft)
Spread: 60-75cm (2-2½ft)
Cultivation: Any good well-drained garden soil and a position in good light suit Oriental Poppies. Remove all dead flowers.
Propagation: The easiest way to increase Oriental Poppies is by lifting and dividing congested plants during spring. Alternatively, sow seeds thinly during summer, 6mm (¼in) deep, in a well-prepared seedbed outdoors. When the seedlings are large enough to handle, thin them to 15cm (6in) apart. In autumn or spring, transfer them to their flowering positions.

Phlox paniculata

(Phlox decussata)
Phlox (UK)
Perennial Phlox · Summer
Perennial Phlox · Fall Phlox (USA)

A well-known and reliable herbaceous perennial for borders, which produces abundant displays of dense 10-15cm (4-6in) heads of 2.5cm (1in) wide flowers from mid to late summer above mid-green, lance-shaped leaves. The range of colours is wide, from white to purple, and red and pink forms include 'Vintage Wine' (claret red), 'Starfire' (deep red), 'Fairy's Petticoat' (shell-pink), 'Windsor' (clear carmine), 'Mother of Pearl' (pink), 'Pinafore Pink' (bright pink), 'Prospero' (pale lilac), and 'Red Indian' (deep crimson).
Height: Range of varieties from 60cm to 1.2m (2-4ft)
Spread: Range of varieties from 45 to 60cm (1½-2ft)
Cultivation: A fertile, well-drained but moisture-retentive soil in full sun or light shade assures success. Give the plants a mulch of well-decomposed compost or manure in spring to help reduce the loss of moisture from the soil. During dry summers, water the soil. In exposed areas, support the plants with twiggy sticks, and in autumn cut down the plants to soil level to tidy them up.

Propagation: Phlox are often infested with microscopic worm-like creatures called eelworms. Although these plants can be increased easily by lifting and dividing congested clumps in spring or autumn and replanting the young outside parts, if the parent plants are infested the new plants will also have the same problem. In such circumstances, it is better to propagate by taking root cuttings in winter or early spring. Cut the thicker roots into 12mm (½in) pieces and place in loam-based compost at 13°C (55°F). Cover the compost lightly. When shoots from these roots are 6.5cm (2½in) high, move the boxes to a cold frame to harden off. Plant out into nursery rows in late spring and leave for a couple of years before transplanting to the permanent site. Herbaceous phloxes can be grown from seeds, but named forms will not breed true However, if you like to experiment when raising plants, phloxes can be easily grown by sowing seeds in loam-based compost during late spring. Place the sown boxes in a cold frame. Prick off the seedlings into further boxes when large enough to handle, and when growing strongly plant out into a well-prepared nursery bed. Set out in the garden during the autumn of the following year.

Left: **Papaver orientale**
Few herbaceous perennials capture as many early to mid-summer glances as this Oriental Poppy. There are several varieties available, in a wide colour range.

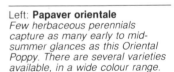

Right: **Phlox paniculata**
'Vintage Wine' This claret-red variety is one of the best known forms of this beautiful herbaceous perennial for herbaceous or mixed borders.

Far right: **Polygonum amplexicaule**
'Atrosanguinea' This herbaceous perennial gives a ground-covering of deep green leaves with spires of red flowers.

Papaver orientale needs a rustic, cottage-garden setting to show off its charms — it never looks as good in a formal setting. When allowed to splay outwards over an old brick path, it is a delight.

Polygonum amplexicaule 'Atrosanguinea'

Mountain Fleece (USA)

A beautiful Himalayan herbaceous perennial with deep green, heart-shaped, long and tapering, pointed leaves. This form displays 15cm (6in) long spikes of red flowers during mid-summer and early autumn. The form 'Firetail' creates attractive bright crimson-scarlet spikes, while 'Inverleith' which grows to 30cm (1ft) bears red poker-like flowers on leafy mounds. The form *P. amplexicaule* 'Pendula', also sold as *Polygonum* 'Arum Gem', displays branching stems bearing dangling tassels of bright pink flowers from mid-summer to autumn. The plant is ideal for a small garden.

Height: 90cm-1.2m (3-4ft)
Spread: 60-75cm (2-2½ft)
Cultivation: Fertile, moist soil in full sun or partial shade is needed. After flowering, cut down the stems to soil-level.
Propagation: This plant is best increased by lifting and dividing the more congested clumps in autumn or spring.

Polygonum bistorta, the Snakeweed or Bistort, is another widely-grown species, mainly in the variety 'Superbum'. It is a mat-forming plant with light green leaves and spikes of pink flowers.

Potentilla atrosanguinea

Himalayan Cinquefoil (UK and USA)

A delightful Himalayan herbaceous perennial; the original form is little grown itself but it has given rise to a wide range of hybrids. They have grey-green, somewhat strawberry-like leaves, with the flowers borne in loose sprays of single or double flowers in heads up to 45cm (1½ft) wide, from mid to late summer. Varieties to look for include 'Flamenco' (large, single, intense red flowers), 'Gibson's Scarlet' (single, brilliant-red) and 'Glory of Nancy' (semi-double, crimson-maroon).

Height: 45-60cm (1½-2ft)
Spread: 38-45cm (15-18in)
Cultivation: Potentillas will do well in a fertile, well-drained soil in full sun. Each spring, mulch them with well-rotted manure or compost, and in dry weather water the plants thoroughly.
Propagation: The easiest way for a home gardener to increase them is by lifting and dividing large clumps in spring or autumn.

Above: **Potentilla atrosanguinea 'Gibson's Scarlet'** *The single brilliant-red flowers of this distinctive herbaceous perennial are a joy from mid to late summer. The strawberry-like leaves supply an ideal foil for the flowers.*

Left: **Sedum spectabile 'Autumn Joy'** *This is one of the easiest to grow and amenable of all garden plants, never failing to create interest through its autumn heads of salmon-pink flowers.*

Sedum spectabile

Ice Plant (UK)

This is one of the most reliable and attractive of all border perennials. It probably gains its common name Ice Plant from its glistening, blue-grey foliage. During late summer and autumn, it bears dense 7.5-15cm (3-6in) wide heads of pink

Potentilla nepalensis has also produced some superb herbaceous perennials, like 'Roxana' (pink, brown-red and orange flowers) and 'Miss Willmott' (cherry pink). Both are 60cm (2ft) high.

Sedum spectabile mixes well with several blue plants, such as rose-purple colchicums and the stiff, upright spires of violet bead-like flowers borne by *Lirope muscari*, the Lily Turf.

flowers flushed with a mauve tinge. Several superb forms are available; perhaps the best known is 'Autumn Joy' with flowers that change from pale rose to a beautiful salmon-pink. 'Carmine' has bright carmine flower heads, 'Meteor' deep carmine-red heads and 'Brilliant' deep rose ones. As a bonus, they are attractive to bees.

Height: 30-45cm (1-1½ft)
Spread: 45cm (1½ft)
Cultivation: Any ordinary well-drained soil and a position in full sun are suitable. Set new plants in position during spring or autumn. In spring, remove the dead flower heads.
Propagation: The easiest way for a home gardener to increase sedums is by lifting and dividing established clumps in spring or autumn. Alternatively, take stem cuttings 2.5-7.5cm (1-3in) long in late spring and insert them in pots of sandy compost in a cold frame.

Schizostylis coccinea

Kaffir Lily (UK)
Crimson Flag · Kaffir Lily (USA)

A well-known South African rhizomatous-rooted herbaceous perennial with mid-green, sword-like leaves and long stems bearing star-shaped 4cm (1½in) wide rich crimson flowers in late autumn and early winter. The flowers are arranged in spikes about 15cm (6in) long. The form 'Major' displays extra-large red flowers on strong stems, 'November Cheer' has pink flowers, 'Viscountess Byng' bears pale pink blooms, and 'Mrs. Hegarty' pale pink flowers.
Height: 60-90cm (2-3ft)
Spread: 30-38cm (12-15in)
Cultivation: Moist, fertile soil and a position in full sun are essential. It is vital that the soil is kept moist, so each spring give it a mulch of compost or peat. In autumn, cut the plants down to soil-level.
Propagation: During spring, lift the plants and divide them into pieces, each containing five or six shoots. Replant these pieces before their roots become dry.

Above: **Schizostylis coccinea 'Major'** *This vivid-red South African plant needs moist, fertile soil. As well as providing late season flowers for the garden it is ideal for use as a cut-flower.*

Schizostylis coccinea is in flower at the same time as the Michaelmas Daisy *Aster novi-belgii.* Soft blue asters blend well with schizostylis, and with silver-leaved *Santolina chamaecyparissus.*

THE FLOWER BORDER

Sidalcea malviflora

Checkerbloom (USA)

An erect, slender, rather twiggy-stemmed hardy herbaceous perennial from Western North America. The mid-green lower leaves are roundish, with five to nine shallow lobes. The funnel-shaped, 5cm (2in) wide, mallow-like pink flowers appear in clustered spires towards the tops of the stems from mid to late summer. Several forms are available, including 'Croftway Red' (deep rich red), 'Loveliness' (shell-pink), 'Nimmerdor' (tapering spires of deep pink flowers), 'Oberon' (clear pink), 'Rose Queen' (rose-pink) and 'William Smith' (warm salmon-pink).
Height: 75cm-1.2m (2½-4ft)
Spread: 45-60cm (1½-2ft)
Cultivation: Ordinary garden soil suits this plant, but it must not be in full sun or strong shade. A position with light speckled shade in soil that does not dry out during summer is ideal. Twiggy sticks are needed to support the plants.
Propagation: It is easily increased by lifting and dividing congested clumps in mid-spring, replanting only the pieces from around the outside. It can be increased from seeds sown in spring in a cold frame, but named forms do not come true in this way.

Above: **Tigridia pavonia 'Rubra'**
The beautiful plant is only half-hardy and requires a warm position. It produces a succession of vividly coloured flowers, each lasting only a day but followed by others to give colour over a long period. The strange markings and spots on the flowers amply justify the plant's common name Tiger Flower.

Left: **Sidalcea malviflora**
The mallow-like pink flowers of this herbaceous perennial are borne on tall stems. After the delicately coloured flowers have faded cut down the stems to 23cm (9in) of soil-level to encourage the development of lateral shoots.

Tigridia pavonia

Tiger Flower · Peacock Tiger Flower · Flower of the Aztecs (UK) Tiger Flower · Shell Flower · One-day Lily (USA)

This is one of the brightest and most eye-catching of all summer-flowering bulbous plants. Originating from Mexico and Peru, it is only half-hardy. The long sword-like mid-green pleated leaves grow up to 60cm (2ft) high. From mid-summer to autumn, it produces 10cm (4in) wide yellow flowers spotted with crimson-brown. These are formed of three large petals and three small ones. Each of these flowers lasts for one day, but fortunately each stem

Sidalcea malvaeflora, with its delicate pink flowers, needs careful positioning in a border if it is not to be dominated by strong colours. An old brick wall provides an attractive background.

Tigridia pavonia does not grow too well with other plants: its colour and shape are dominant and can all too easily overwhelm other plants. It is best grown against a warm wall and given a spot to itself.

Above: **Tulip 'Trance'**
This Division 3 *tulip has startling coloured flowers in mid-spring. It prefers a sunny position where there is some lime in the soil. 'Van der Eerden' is another superb red tulip in this division.*

Tulips

The range of these much-loved spring bulbs is extensive. They can be used in bedding schemes during spring, or in mixed borders, rock gardens, tubs and troughs, as well as indoors during winter and early spring. There is a wide range of species, and in addition botanists have classified those that have been created by bulb experts. There are many different divisions, encompassing the wide range of flower sizes, shapes and heights. These are:

Division 1: Single Early
(15-38cm/6-15in): The single flowers appear in spring when grown outdoors, or during winter indoors. Each flower is 7.5-13cm (3-5in) wide and sometimes opens flat when in direct and full sun. Many varieties are available, including some fine red and pink ones, as well as white, yellow, orange and purple.

Division 2: Double Early
(30-38cm/12-15in): The double flowers appear in spring when grown out-of-doors in bedding schemes, or earlier when forced indoors. Each flower is 10cm (4in) wide and rather like a double paeony. The colour range is wide, including pink and red.

bears up to eight flowers. Several forms are available in red or scarlet, such as 'Liliacea' (reddish-purple with white variegations), 'Rubra' (orange-red with red and yellow spotted centres) and 'Speciosa' (scarlet with yellow and red centres). *Tigridia pavonia* is only one of a genus formed of about twelve species, all coming chiefly from Mexico but some also from Guatemala.Except for the Tiger Flower, which is descriptively known as the Jockey Cap in New Zealand, they are rarely grown in Britain and really need the benefit of a frost-proof greenhouse, although they can be planted outdoors in spring and lifted for storage in a frost-proof place during autumn.

Height: 45-60cm (1½-2ft)
Spread: 20-25cm (8-10in)
Cultivation: Rich, well-drained soil and a warm, sunny position are best. Plant the bulbs 7.5cm (3in) deep during spring, and after flowering lift and store them in a frost-free and vermin-proof place during winter. Only in exceptionally warm areas and when grown against a west or south-facing wall can the bulbs be left in position during winter.
Propagation: When the plants are lifted and divided in autumn, detach the young offsets from around the sides of the mother plants and re-plant them separately during the warmer spring weather.

Blue, scarlet and gold mixtures can be created by a carpet planting of a pale blue Forget-me-not (*Myosotis*) and a planting of the scarlet and gold single early tulip 'Keizerskroon'.

THE FLOWER BORDER

Above: **Tulip 'Aladdin'**
A lily-flowered tulip from Division 7, with a typical waisted appearance and pointed petals. 'Dyanito' is another lily-flowered tulip in this division, and 'Queen of Sheba' is red, with orange edges.

Division 3: Mendel
(38-50cm/15-20in): These flower later than the previous types, with rounded, 10-13cm (4-5in) wide flowers on quite slender stems. Colours include white and red, as well as yellow. They look like a cross between single early types and Darwins.

Division 4: Triumph (up to 50cm/20in): These bear angular-shaped, 10-13cm (4-5in) wide flowers on strong stems in mid-spring. Colours include yellow, gold and lilac, as well as pink and red.

Division 5: Darwin Hybrids
(60-75cm/2-2½ft): These are among the most large flowered and brilliant of all tulips, with flowers up to 18cm (7in) wide during mid-spring. There are multi-coloured forms, as well as orange, purple, yellow and red varieties.

Division 6: Darwin
(60-75cm/2-2½ft): These are widely used in bedding schemes, producing rounded flowers up to

13cm (5in) wide in late spring. Varieties are available in white, yellow and purple, as well as multi-colours and pink and red.

Division 7: Lily-flowered
(45-60cm/1½-2ft): These are characterized by the narrow waists of the flowers, also the pointed petals that curl outwards, reaching 20cm (8in) wide during mid-spring. They look distinctive when massed in a bedding scheme. Colours include white, orange, yellow and multicoloured forms, as well as shades of red.

Division 8: Cottage (up to 90cm/3ft): This old grouping has

oval or rounded flowers 10-13cm (4-5in) wide in mid-spring. The petals sometimes have a hint of fringing at their tips, and are looser than in other forms. Flower colours include white, pink, yellow, lilac and green, as well as red.

Division 9: Rembrandt
(75cm/2½ft): These are tulips with 'broken' colours. The rounded, 13cm (5cm) wide flowers have vivid splashes of colour on the petals during mid-spring. Base colours include white, orange, yellow, pink, violet and brown, as well as red, with eye-catching broken colours superimposed.

For a **yellow, orange-red and blue mixture** try a deep blue Forget-me-not (*Myosotis*), orange-red 'President Hoover' and the yellow 'Mrs. John T. Scheepers'. Both of these are in Division 8.

Above: **Tulip 'Orajezon'**
A superb Division 6 tulip used in bedding schemes where it flowers in late spring. Tulips in this division are probably the most widely grown and popular for setting in spring bedding displays.

flat, giving the appearance of a water-lily. They open in spring on sturdy stems, and are ideal for fronts of borders, rock gardens and containers. Most have two-coloured flowers.

Division 13: Fosteriana varieties (45cm/1½ft): These are derived from *Tulipa fosteriana* and produce large blunt-ended flowers in red and yellow in mid-spring.

Division 14: Greigii varieties (25cm/10in): These are mainly derived from *Tulipa greigii*, bearing brilliant, long-lasting red, yellow and near-white flowers in mid-spring. The petals reach 7.5cm long when the flowers are fully open.

Cultivation: When grown in the garden, select well-drained soil, preferably facing south and in a sheltered position. Set the bulbs 15cm (6in) deep during early winter. Space them 10-15cm (4-6in) apart. Remove dead flowers and dig up the bulbs when the leaves turn yellow. However, if the bed is needed earlier, dig up the bulbs as soon as flowering is over and heel them into a trench until the foliage has yellowed and died down.

Division 10: Parrot (45-60cm/1½-2ft): These have flowers up to 20cm (8in) wide, easily recognizable by their feather-like and heavily-fringed petals, appearing in mid-spring. The colour range includes brilliant white, orange, yellow and purple, as well as red and pink.

Division 11: Double Late (45-60cm/1½-2ft): These have very large and showy double flowers, somewhat resembling paeonies and up to 20cm (8in) wide. They remain in flower for a long period during mid-spring. Colours include white, orange, yellow and violet, as

Above: **Tulip 'Ida'**
A Division 4 tulip with a yellow base dramatically streaked red. This Triumph tulip flowers in mid-spring and thrives in full sun. Other Triumph tulips include 'Rose Korneforos' (rose-red) and 'Edith Eddy' (red with white edges).

well as pink and red. Also, some are multi-coloured, with stripes and edgings.

Division 12: Kaufmanniana varieties (10-15cm/4-10in): These have been developed from *Tulipa kaufmanniana*, and have fine-pointed flowers that open nearly

For a **blue and red spring-bedding mixture**, perhaps at the top of a dry stone wall, try blue *Aubrieta deltoidea* and the Division 13 tulip 'Red Emperor', a tulip derived from *Tulipa fosteriana*.

THE FLOWER BORDER

Propagation: The easiest way is to remove off-set bulbs clustered at the bases of the bulbs. These can be planted in a nursery bed to develop into flowering-sized bulbs.

Right: **Tulip 'Allegretto'**
This double late tulip from Division 11 *is flamboyant, with long-lasting flowers during spring. 'Brilliant Fire' displays red flowers, and has the benefit of being scented.*

Below right: **Tulip 'Flaming Parrot'**
An exciting Division 10 *tulip with a yellow and white background vividly striped red. Many Parrot tulips are bicoloured, and when fully open may measure up to 20cm (8in) wide.*

Below: **Tulipa greigii**
A superb species tulip with grey-green lance-shaped and distinctively veined leaves. The blunt-pointed orange-scarlet flowers appear in mid-spring. It is the parent of many hybrids in Division 14, and itself is well worthy of a prominent position in a rock garden.

For a **salmon, orange-red and yellow mixture** try a carpet of the salmon *Cheiranthus cheiri* 'Easter Queen' and a mixture of the orange-red 'President Hoover' and the yellow 'Mrs. John T. Scheepers'.

Above: **Tulip 'Greenland'**
A demure tulip from Division 8 *that reveals green stripes on a pink background. Other outstandingly attractive pink Cottage tulips include 'Palestrina' (salmon-pink) and 'Mirella' (deep salmon-pink).*

Further plants to consider

Anemone x hybrida
(Anemone japonica · Anemone x elegans)

Height: 60-90cm (2-3ft)   Spread: 30-45cm (1-1½ft)
A hardy herbaceous perennial with several pink forms, including 'September Charm' (clear pink), 'Queen Charlotte' (semi-double and pink) and 'Max Vogel' (pink).

Bergenia cordifolia
Height: 30cm (1ft)   Spread: 30-38cm (12-15in)
A well-known hardy herbaceous perennial with large, mid-green, leathery leaves and lilac-rose flowers in dome-shaped heads during spring. The hybrid 'Ballawley' bears large red flowers.

Centranthus ruber
(Kentranthus ruber)

Height: 45-90cm (1½-3ft)   Spread: 30-38cm (12-15in)
A hardy herbaceous perennial with long, strong stems displaying star-shaped, deep pink or red flowers from mid to late summer. Unfortunately, the leaves have an unpleasant smell when crushed, so set it to the back or middle of the border.

Geum x borisii
Height: 30cm (1ft)   Spread: 30-38cm (12-15in)
A beautiful hardy herbaceous perennial bearing 2.5cm (1in) wide orange-scarlet flowers during early summer and often intermittently into late summer.

Monarda didyma
Oswego Tea · Bee Balm · Sweet Bergamot (UK and USA)
Height: 60-90cm (2-3ft)   Spread: 45cm (1½ft)
A hardy herbaceous perennial with beautiful whorled heads of flowers from mid-summer to early autumn. Pink and red forms include 'Cambridge Scarlet' (bright scarlet), 'Croftway Pink' (rose-pink), 'Melissa' (pale pink) and 'Pillar Box' (bright red).

Pyrethrum roseum
Height: 60-75cm (2-2½ft)   Spread: 45cm (1½ft)
A spectacular hardy herbaceous perennial displaying bright green, feathery leaves. During mid-summer it bears 5-6.5cm (2-2½in) wide, daisy-like, single or double flowers. Pink and red forms include 'Brenda' (single, cerise-pink), 'Bressingham Red' (single, crimson-scarlet), 'Eileen May Robinson' (single, clear pink), 'Kelway's Glorious' (single, crimson-red), 'J.N. Twerdy' (double, deep red), 'Madeleine' (double, clear pink) and 'Venus' (double, shell-pink).

Verbascum x hybridum 'Pink Domino'
Mullein (UK and USA)
Height: 90cm-1.2m (3-4ft)   Spread: 38-45cm (15-18in)
A superb hardy hybrid herbaceous perennial with beautiful deep rose-pink flowers during mid to late summer.

If you like a **yellow and scarlet and gold mixture** try
the stunning combination of a planting of
a yellow viola and the scarlet and gold 'Keizerskroon'.
The latter is a single early tulip from Division 1.

CHAPTER TWO

ROCK AND NATURALIZED GARDENS

Rock gardens create homes for some of the most delicate and diminutive of all garden plants. They become miniature gardens on their own, with legions of dedicated enthusiasts who avidly search garden literature for new species or fresh forms. Some of the requirements for a successful rock garden are good drainage, plenty of light and a site that is not overcast with deciduous trees which would shed their leaves over the delicate plants in autumn. This can be achieved by constructing a raised site, either on a slope or a well-drained artificial mound, but even if this is not available, retaining walls, paths formed of natural paving stone and natural stone sinks can create attractive homes for rock garden plants.

Red and pink plants for setting between natural paving slabs include the New Zealand Burr *Acaena microphylla*, with crimson burrs; *Antennaria dioica* 'Nyewood', with crimson flowers, as well as the form 'Rosea' bearing deep pink heads; *Erinus alpinus*, with bright starry pink flowers; and *Thymus drucei*, often better known as *T. serpyllum*, with flowers variable from deep red, through pink to white. The form 'Annie Hall' displays pale pink flowers, while 'Coccineus' is crimson.

Plants for setting in cracks in walls as well as cascading from their tops usually exhibit more of a trailing and cascading nature, although a balance is needed between those that cascade and those that just peep out of cracks. A dominant and spreading candidate is *Helianthemum nummularium* 'Beech Park Scarlet' with crimson-scarlet flowers rarely failing to attract attention.

Candidates for troughs and stone sinks need to be selected with care: those with a propensity for suffocating their neighbours should certainly be barred from candidacy for a sink. Hybrids of *Lewisia cotyledon* are superb, while the Cobweb Houseleek *Sempervivum arachnoideum*, with an attractive globular rosette of leaves and bright rose-red flowers, is another delight. There are, of course, many other outstandingly attractive and slow-growing plants with red or pink flowers for sink gardens; a selection of the best is fully described and illustrated in this chapter.

Left: **Rock Roses (Helianthemum nummalarium)** *are shrubby and low-growing plants, ideal for setting at the edge of a border to soften the path's edges.*

ROCK AND NATURALIZED GARDENS

Above: **Androsace primuloides 'Chumbyi'**
This is a delightful rock garden plant with beautiful clear pink flowers during mid-spring to mid-summer. It is essential that the rosettes are kept relatively dry during winter.

Androsace primuloides

(Androsace sarmentosa)
Rock Jasmine (UK and USA)

A hardy rock garden perennial with silky white, woolly, narrow, lance-shaped, mid-green leaves. The rosettes of rose-pink flowers are borne on 5-10cm (2-4in) stems from mid-spring to mid-summer. The form 'Chumbyi' has clear pink flowers, while 'Watkinsii' bears highly attractive rosy-red flowers.
Height: 10-13cm (4-5in)
Spread: 38-60cm (15-24in)
Cultivation: Good drainage and a sunny position are essential. Preferably, the soil should contain coarse sand or limestone grit. Set the plants in position during spring. Wet soil encourages the leaves to rot, and in very wet areas protection with cloches may be necessary during winter.
Propagation: This is quite easily achieved by potting up rooted rosettes at the edges of the main clump in early autumn. Stand the pots in an open but sheltered part of the garden during winter. Protect them from excessive rain as necessary and plant out into the garden during spring.

Below: **Anthyllis montana**
This European alpine needs full sun and a well-drained gritty soil. Once established, it is best left alone, as its tap-root system resents any disturbance.

Androsace lanuginosa, from the Himalayas, is a delightful trailing and mat-forming Rock Jasmine, with silver-green leaves and pinkish flowers in mid-summer and autumn. It is ideal for drystone walls.

Armeria juniperifolia

(Armeria caespitosa)
Thrift (UK and USA)

This hardy evergreen perennial from Spain is one of the best known rock garden plants, producing stiff grass-like, grey-green leaves in tufted clumps. The 12-18mm (½-¾in) wide, tightly packed, pink flower-heads are borne singly at the tops of 5-7.5cm (2-3in) long stems during late spring and early summer. The form 'Bevan's Variety' is widely grown and displays deep pink flowers on 2.5-5cm (1-2in) stems.
Height: 5-7.5cm (2-3in)
Spread: 20-25cm (8-10in)
Cultivation: Any good well-drained garden soil suits thrift, and it likes a position in full sun. Set the plants in position during spring or autumn. As soon as the flowers fade, clip them off to make the plants neat for the rest of the year.
Propagation: This is easily done by lifting and dividing large clumps in spring. Replant them immediately. Alternatively, 5cm (2in) basal cuttings can be taken in late summer and inserted in equal parts peat and sharp sand.

Anthyllis montana

Mountain Kidney Vetch (UK)

An unusual rock garden plant that forms a low woody bush with hairy foliage, giving it a silvery appearance. During mid-summer it bears red or red-purple flowers at the stem ends.
Height: 20-30cm (8-12in)
Spread: 38-45cm (15-18in)
Cultivation: Anthyllis prefers a well-drained gritty soil and a sunny site. It will tolerate a limestone soil.
Propagation: During summer, take 5-7.5cm (2-3in) long cuttings with heels. Insert them in pots containing a sandy compost and put them in a cold frame. It is difficult to raise from seeds, but these can be sown in early spring and placed in a cold frame. Once planted, it is best left alone as it resents disturbance.

Above: **Armeria juniperifolia 'Bevan's Variety'**
A reliable and neat tufted rock garden plant that flowers in early summer, armeria also grows well in a stone sink. The flowers and foliage can be enhanced by covering the soil with clean shingle.

Below: **Armeria maritima 'Bloodstone'**
This species is related to the slightly smaller Armeria juniperifolia and rises to 15-25cm (6-10in). Again it is deal for rock gardens or for setting at the edges of a border. This variety produces glowing crimson flowers.

Armeria pseudarmeria, often better known as *A. plantaginea*, grows much larger than *A. lanuginosa*, to a height of 60cm (2ft) and a spread of 38cm (15in). The variety 'Bees Ruby' has bright ruby red flowers.

Astilbe x arendsii

False Goat's Beard (UK)
Perennial Spiraea (USA)

This beautiful hardy herbaceous hybrid perennial has *Astilbe chinensis davidii* in its parentage and comes in a colour range from purple-red to nearly white. Many pink and red forms are available, flowering from mid to late summer. Varieties to look for include 'Bressingham Beauty' (rich pink and free-flowering), 'Fanal' (intense deep red), 'Red Sentinel' (intense brick red), 'Rheinland' (rich pink) and 'Federsee' (rose-red).

Height: 60-90cm (2-3ft)
Spread: 38-50cm (15-20in)
Cultivation: Astilbes prefer fertile, moisture-retentive soil in full sun or light shade. In dry seasons it may be necessary to water the plants. Applying a mulch helps to conserve moisture in the soil. In autumn, cut the foliage down to soil-level.
Propagation: Lifting and dividing established clumps every three or four years in spring is the easiest method. Do not let the roots dry out when dividing them. Replant them immediately so that the roots do not become dry.

Above left: **Astilbe x arendsii**
This beautiful hardy herbaceous plant has feathery spires of flowers from mid to late summer. It is ideal for a moist area in the garden. It is best planted in large drifts where it creates a dominant display for much of the summer.

Above: **Astilbe chinensis 'Pumila'**
Most astilbes like to grow by the side of a pool, but this diminutive form does well in drier conditions. During summer it develops fluffy pink spires that display themselves above the foliage, never failing to produce an exciting spectacle.

Astilbes are an ideal choice for the moist surrounds of informal garden pools. The red and pink forms blend well with yellow hemerocallis and the large blue heads of *Hydrangea macrophylla.*

Astilbe chinensis 'Pumila'

Without a doubt, this miniature astilbe is a treasure in a rock garden. Its herbaceous perennial nature ensures fresh, mid-green, fern-like foliage each year, with 23cm (9in) long spires of fluffy pink flowers flushed purple appearing from mid-summer to autumn.
Height: 23-30cm (9-12in)
Spread: 30-38cm (12-15in)
Cultivation: Relatively moist and fertile soil in full sun or light shade suit this plant. The roots like a cool position, for example by the side of a rock that affords a shady and cool root run. In autumn cut the plants down to soil-level.
Propagation: It is most easily increased by lifting and dividing clumps every three or four years and replanting them 25-30cm (10-12in) apart. Do this in mid-spring and water well until the plants are established.

Cornus alba

Red-barked Dogwood (UK)
Tartarian Dogwood · Tatarian Dogwood (USA)

This hardy, vigorous, wide-spreading, deciduous shrub belongs to a group loosely known as Dogwoods or Cornels. This particular species has a suckering habit and produces masses of upright stems. The current year's stems are bright red in winter. All these are suitable for a wild or naturalized garden.
Height: 2.1-2.7m (7-9ft)
Spread: 1.8-3m (6-10ft)
Cultivation: Rich, moist soil and full sun suit these shrubs best. During spring, cut down the stems to within a few inches of the soil to encourage the development of shoots that will display good rich colour in late summer and winter.
Propagation: It is easily increased by layering long shoots in autumn. Alternatively, take hardwood cuttings in autumn, inserting them in trenches with sand along their bases to prevent waterlogging.

Above: **Cornus alba 'Sibirica'** *This distinctively bright-stemmed shrub makes an impressive picture during winter. To obtain highly-coloured shoots, the previous season's growth must be cut down nearly to soil-level in spring.*

Astilbe chinensis 'Pumila' with its upright spires can create the effect of sudden height in a rock garden. It often looks good by a drystone wall, whose colour and texture complement the flowers.

Cornus alba 'Sibirica' looks best in a site where low-angled winter sun will catch the stems. It makes an ideal companion for daffodils, which will provide colour to hide its stems when cut down in spring.

ROCK AND NATURALIZED GARDENS

Daphne cneorum

Garland Flower (UK and USA)

This is a beautiful and highly scented ground-hugging and spreading evergreen shrub from Central and Southern Europe, ideal for a rock garden. The wiry stems are well clothed with narrow, deep green leaves, and the 12mm (½in) wide rose-pink flowers appear during early summer. The form 'Eximia' boasts deeper pink flowers and is slightly larger.

Height: 16cm (6in)
Spread: 75cm-1.3m (2½-4½ft)
Cultivation: Daphnes like a well-drained but moisture-retentive garden soil in full sun or slight shade. They tolerate lime in the soil. As the roots need to be kept cool, mulch with well-rotted compost in spring. If the plants spread too much in one direction, prune them back carefully after flowering.
Propagation: The easiest way for a home gardener to increase this plant is by layering shoots in autumn. Alternatively, take 5-10cm (2-4in) long heel cuttings in mid to late summer and insert them in pots containing equal parts peat and sharp sand, placed in a cold frame. When the plants are rooted, pot them up into loam-based compost, setting them out in the garden about eighteen months later into their final positions.

Left: **Daphne cneorum**
One of the most beautiful and pleasantly-scented of all garden plants, this daphne will spread up to 1.3m (4½ft) wide. The four-petalled rose-pink flowers appear during early summer.

Dianthus pavonius

(Dianthus neglectus · Dianthus alpinus)

This attractive but variable hardy rock garden plant forms neat hummocks of narrow grey-green leaves. During mid to late summer these are smothered with pale pink to deep crimson 3cm (1¼in) wide flowers on short stems 2.5cm (1in) long.
Height: 10-20cm (4-8in)
Spread: 15-20cm (6-8in)
Cultivation: Ordinary well-drained garden soil and a sunny position assure success. Sprinkling stone chippings over the surface helps to prevent heavy rain storms splashing soil on to the plants. The chippings also improve surface drainage.
Propagation: During mid-summer take 7.5-10cm (3-4in) long cuttings and insert them in pots containing equal parts peat and sharp sand. Place these in a cold frame. When rooted, pot the plants up into loam-based compost in small pots and replace in the frame. When established, plant out into the garden.

Below: **Dianthus pavonius**
This dainty rock garden plant is often better known as Dianthus neglectus. *During summer it displays fringed pale pink to deep crimson flowers.*

Daphne cneorum is very adaptable and mixes well with many other plants. Try growing tall St Bernard's Lily (*Anthericum liliago*) behind, with silver-leaved *Europs acraeus* on one side.

Left: **Erinus alpinus**
This beautiful and highly adaptable plant lives happily in a rock garden or on a dry stone wall. It seeds itself readily, rapidly producing a supply of fresh plants.

Right: **Fritillaria imperialis**
This distinctive and eye-catching spring-flowering bulb produces an impressive stem bearing bell-shaped flowers. The tuft of leaves at the top of the stem creates the impression of a crown.

Fritillaria imperialis

Crown Imperial (UK and USA)

This familiar, vigorous and distinctive plant from the Himalayas produces stiff, upright stems with wavy lance-shaped glossy green leaves partly clasping them. During spring, it bears dense clusters of bell-shaped 5cm (2in) long flowers at the tops of the stems. These range from yellow to rich red. Above the flowers is a cluster of partially erect leaves, resembling a crown. It is just as attractive in large drifts in a naturalized or woodland garden as in a formal setting, perhaps alongside a path.

Height: 60-90cm (2-3ft)
Spread: 30-38cm (12-15in)
Cultivation: Fritillarias require fertile, well-drained soil in full or light shade. As the fleshy bulbs are easily damaged, they are best planted 20cm (8in) deep during autumn and left in one position for several years. Setting the bulbs on their sides prevents water rotting their tops. In heavy soils, put a handful of sharp sand under each bulb. During autumn, cut down the stems to soil-level.
Propagation: Fritillarias can be grown from seed, but this method takes up to six years to produce flowering-sized bulbs, so it is better to propagate from offsets taken from the parent bulb in late summer. Plant them in a nursery bed for two years before transferring them to their final flowering positions.

Erinus alpinus

A hardy though relatively short-lived dwarf evergreen perennial for rock gardens or dry stone walls. It also does well between natural paving slabs. The spoon-shaped, mid-green leaves are deeply toothed and borne in low, tufted mounds with bright pink 6mm (¼in) wide, star-shaped flowers from early spring to late summer. The form 'Mrs Charles Boyle' has deep pink flowers, while 'Dr Hanele' produces attractive carmine blooms.
Height: 7.5cm (3in)
Spread: 15-20cm (6-8in)
Cultivation: Well-drained soil is essential, as is a sunny position.
Propagation: Erinus seeds itself quite readily, and even the cultivated forms come true when grown from seed.

Erinus alpinus is a delight when allowed to fill the gaps in natural stone paths, in harmony with antennarias, *Helichrysum bellidioides, Mazus repens, Mentha requienii* and *Valeriana montana.*

Fritillaria imperialis is ideal for naturalizing with other plants, like miniature tulips and violas, in a wild garden. However, it also does well in narrow beds in small, more formal gardens.

ROCK AND NATURALIZED GARDENS

Geranium dalmaticum

This neat Yugoslavian and Albanian Crane's-bill is a densely foliaged herbaceous perennial with deeply-lobed, rather palm-like, mid-green, flossy leaves that take on gorgeous tints in autumn. During mid to late summer it bears 2.5cm (1in) wide, demure pink, five-petalled, saucer-shaped flowers on stems 10-13cm (4-5in) long.
Height: 15cm (6in)
Spread: 25-30cm (10-12in)
Cultivation: Any well-drained garden soil in full sun or partial shade is suitable. In autumn, cut down the plant to soil-level.
Propagation: It is easily increased by lifting and dividing clumps in spring or autumn. It is quite easy to split up the plants. If some of them are rather small, pot them up into small pots and allow them to establish themselves properly before setting them out in the rock garden in their permanent positions.

Left: **Geranium dalmaticum**
A dainty Crane's-bill for a rock garden, this species has mid-green leaves that take on lovely red and orange tints in autumn. These form a bonus to the soft pink flowers.

Gypsophila repens

(Gypsophila prostrata)

This pretty mat-forming, wiry-stemmed, trailing alpine gypsophila with narrow grey-green leaves looks superb when clothed with 9mm (⅓in) wide pink or white flowers throughout the summer. The form 'Letchworth Rose' is a delightful pink, while 'Dorothy Teacher' bears bluish-grey leaves and clear pink flowers.
Height: 10-15cm (4-6in)
Spread: 45-60cm (1½-2ft)
Cultivation: Well-drained, slightly alkaline soil is best, although gypsophilas also do well in acid conditions. They are best positioned to trail over the top of a dry stone wall or large rocks.

Geranium dalmaticum has a flattened-dome shape, making it an ideal choice for the junction of two paths in a rock garden. It is also superb for a terrace or dry stone wall where it can spill over.

Gypsophila aretioides is another alpine species worth growing, with a tight, cushion-forming growth 5cm (2in) high. *G. cerastioides*, 7.5cm (3in) high, has grey leaves and clusters of white flowers.

Propagation: During spring, take 5cm (2in) long cuttings and insert them in pots containing equal parts of peat and sharp sand. Place these in a cold frame. When rooted, pot up the plants into 7.5cm (3in) pots of loam-based compost. They can be planted out in autumn or spring.

Right: **Helianthemum nummularium 'Ben Dearg'**
Few mid-summer-flowering rock plants are as impressive as this low-growing, somewhat sprawling perennial. And even if it does exceed its position, it can easily be trimmed back after flowering.

Below: **Gypsophila repens 'Letchworth Rose'** *This distinctive pink-flowered alpine gypsophila produces a frothy mass of flowers well suited for tumbling over walls and large rocks. Its loose and lax nature when trailing over walls allows the attractive nature of the stone to be seen.*

Helianthemum nummularium

(Helianthemum chamaecistus H. vulgare)
Rock Rose (UK)
Sun Rose · Rock Rose (USA)

This shrubby, low-growing and spreading plant is invaluable in a rock garden. The deep green, narrow, elliptical leaves are borne sparsely on trailing stems, with 12-25mm (½in-1in) wide, saucer-shaped flowers appearing during mid-summer. The colour range is wide, including 'Beech Park Scarlet' (crimson-scarlet), 'Wisley Pink' (pink), 'Ben Dearg' (deep copper-orange) and 'Cerise Queen' (rosy-red).
Height: 10-15cm (4-6in)
Spread: 45-60cm (1½-2ft)
Cultivation: Well-drained garden soil and a sunny position assure success. Do not hesitate to deal with over-rampant plants; they will withstand quite severe pruning after flowering.
Propagation: During mid to late summer take 5-7.5cm (2-3in) long cuttings with 'heels'. Insert them in pots of equal parts peat and sharp sand and place these in a cold frame. Pot up the plants when rooted into small pots of loam-based compost and replace in a cold frame. Plant out into the rock garden in late spring.

Helianthemum nummularium is extremely impressive when trailing over a low wall, so the plant can be seen from above as well as the sides. It is useful for breaking up the stark outline of a wall.

Oxalis adenophylla

This delightful, dainty, low-growing hardy perennial has a fibre-coated bulb-like rootstock, greyish leaves and long-stemmed, solitary, cup-shaped, satiny-pink flowers in early summer.

Height: 6.5-7.5cm (2½-3in)
Spread: 15cm (6in)
Cultivation: A well-drained, light, peat-enriched soil and a sunny position are essential. A light soil covering of well-washed shingle helps to ensure good drainage and an attractive background for the flowers and foliage. The foliage dies down during winter.
Propagation: This can be easily done by separating the bulb offsets in early spring. These can be replanted directly into the rock garden or potted into a gritty compost until healthy young plants become properly established. Another beautiful South American oxalis, but this time for an alpine house, is *O. enneaphylla* 'Rosea'. It is bulbous-rooted, with partially folded grey leaves and pale rose-pink flowers which appear during mid-summer.

Below: **Oxalis adenophylla**
The delicate appearance of this Chilean hardy perennial never fails to add an element of interest to rock gardens.

Parahebe catarractae

This dainty-flowered sub-shrub delights in cascading over and between rocks, displaying its massed terminal heads of flowers, featuring rose-purple lines set on a background of white, during summer. The mid to dark green, lance-shaped to oval leaves with serrated edges are an attractive bonus.

Height: 25-30cm (10-12in)
Spread: 38-45cm (15-18in)
Cultivation: Parahebes delight in a well-drained neutral soil, preferably covered with well-washed shingle and in a sunny position. Set them at the top of the rock garden so

Oxalis adenophylla has delicate colouring, and needs subtly coloured neighbours if it is not to be dominated. It looks at its best when given plenty of space, rather than being hemmed in.

Left: **Penstemon newberryi**
This sprawling and scrambling penstemon produces pink to rose-pink flowers, and there are many other superb penstemons suitable for rock gardens.

Penstemon newberryi

This is a useful bushy semi-evergreen sub-shrub for trailing over rocks and dry stone walls, where its sprawling nature helps to merge the structural elements. Its elongated, 3-4cm (1 ¼-1 ½ in) long, snapdragon-like, pink to rose-pink flowers appear against a carpet of small, mid-green leaves during mid-summer.

Height: 20cm (8in)
Spread: 30-38cm (12-15in)
Cultivation: A well-drained soil is essential. Penstemons flourish in full sun, though a sheltered site may be needed, as the plants will suffer during exceptionally cold winters, despite being generally hardy. Badly drained soils contribute to failure during cold spells. If possible, it is wise to have a stock of small plants ready to replace any that are damaged.
Propagation: Although they can be increased from seed sown during early spring in boxes of loam-based seed compost, the resulting seedlings can be variable. Instead, take 5-7.5cm (2-3in) long cuttings from non-flowering shoots during late summer or early autumn. Insert them in pots containing equal parts peat and sharp sand and put these in a cold frame. When the young plants are rooted, pot them up into loam-based compost and place in a cold frame during winter. Plant out into the garden in late spring. Another attractive alpine species is *P. davidsonii*, a low sub-shrub which grows up to 10cm (4in) high and produces ruby-red flowers in mid-summer.

they can tumble between rocks and benefit from better drainage at the top of a slope.
Propagation: It is easily increased by taking soft cuttings 5-7.5cm (2-3in) long, from mid to late summer. Insert them in pots of sandy compost and place these in a cold frame. When the plants are properly rooted, nip out their growing tips to encourage dense bushy growth.
This species is related to the hebes and veronicas, and very frequently there is some confusion about the identity of plants. To ensure you have the right plants buy only those listed as *Parahebe catarractae*, not *Hebe catarractae*.

Left: **Parahebe catarractae**
This beautiful shrubby plant delights in well-drained soil and a sunny position.

Parahebe catarractae blends well with dainty bright yellow flowers, but beware of overdoing such a combination as the contrast can be overpowering. A good companion is *Sedum acre* 'Aureum'.

Penstemon roezlii, which grows to 15cm (6in) high, is another candidate for the edge of a rock ledge where it can cascade freely. *P. scouleri*, with lavender-blue flowers, is upright and slightly taller.

Saponaria ocymoides

Soapwort · Rock Soapwort (UK)
Soapwort (USA)

This delightful, vigorous, trailing
rock-garden perennial is invaluable
for creating prostrate mats of
colour flowing over rocks or
cascading from dry stone walls. It
produces long, lance-shaped, mid-
green leaves, with five-petalled,
12mm (½in) wide, bright rose-pink
flowers from mid to late summer.
Several excellent forms are
available, such as 'Rubra Compact'
(rich carmine), 'Splendens' (dark
pink) and 'Compacta' which is like
the ordinary type but more
compact.
Height: 7.5cm (3in)
Spread: 30cm (1ft)
Cultivation: Soapworts appreciate
a well-drained fertile garden soil in
full sun or light shade.
Propagation: Plants can be lifted
and divided in autumn or spring.
Alternatively, soft stem cuttings
can be taken in summer from non-
flowering shoots and inserted in
pots of sandy compost, placed in a
cold frame. Pot plants up into
loam-based compost when rooted.

Above: **Saponaria ocymoides**
This delightful rock garden plant
cascades in a spectacular manner
over stone walls and rocks. In
such positions the bright rose-pink
flowers are a delight, appearing
from mid to late summer.

Below: **Saponaria officinalis**
This is the original single-flowered
form, with fragrant rose-pink
flowers borne on erect stems. A
superb double-flowered pink form
is now available, too. It is best
positioned in a wild garden where
its invasive nature does not
interfere with neighbouring plants.

Saponaria officinalis

Soapwort · Bouncing Bet (UK and
USA)

This hardy herbaceous perennial is
a native of Europe and parts of
Asia, and is often found naturalized
in areas in Britain that are or have
been inhabited by humans. The
common name Soapwort refers to
the leaves which, when bruised in
water, create a lather. At one time,
Soapwort was known as Fuller's
Herb; a fuller was a person whose
trade was to cleanse cloth. In the
past it was used to clean old
curtains, although why it was
relegated to such a job is not clear
when it was perfectly efficient on
other cloths.
    The 2.5-4cm (1-1½in) wide
flowers are pink and single and
borne in mid to late summer in
terminal clusters on stiff, upright
stems, clasped by pale-green
leaves. Several attractive forms
are available, such as 'Roseo-
plena', with double pink flowers.
Height: 45-90cm (1½-2ft)
Spread: 60cm (2ft)
Cultivation: Soapwort prefers a
well-drained fertile soil and a
position in full sun or light shade.
In exposed areas it will require
support from twiggy sticks that the
foliage can grow through and hide.
In autumn, cut down the stems to
soil-level.
Propagation: You can take
cuttings in summer, but it is much
easier to increase by lifting and
dividing established clumps in
autumn or spring.

Saponaria ocymoides is such a spectacular plant
when in bloom that the pink flowers can be
dominated by stronger coloured plants nearby, so
take care when planting it in a group.

Saponaria officinalis is known as Bouncing Bet in
North America. In this context, 'bouncing' refers to
the good health and vitality this medicinal herb may
bring; 'Bet' is an abbreviation for Elizabeth.

Above: **Thymus drucei**
This delightful European and British native prostrate sub-shrub is a delight with its fragrant summer flowers, and is invaluable for covering bare soil with colour.

Thymus drucei

(Thymus serpyllum)
Wild Thyme (UK)
Wild Thyme; Lemon Thyme (USA)

Few gardeners do not know this prostrate hardy sub-shrub with narrow, rather spoon-shaped grey-green leaves. The variably coloured flowers — from red to pink and white — appear in small clustered heads from mid to late summer. Several superb forms are available, including 'Annie Hall' (pale pink) and 'Coccineus' (rich crimson).
Height: 4-7.5cm (1½-3in)
Spread: 60-90cm (2-3ft)
Cultivation: Any good, well-drained garden soil in a sunny position suits thyme. To keep the plants neat, use a pair of garden shears to clip off dead flower heads.
Propagation: The easiest way to increase this plant is by lifting and dividing congested clumps in spring or early autumn.

Further plants to consider

Antennaria dioica
Height: 5-30cm (2-12in)   Spread: 30-45cm (1-1½ft)
A hardy evergreen perennial with a creeping habit and white, pink-tipped flowers during early summer. The form 'Nyewood' boasts crimson flowers, while 'Rosea' has deep pink blooms.

Dianthus deltoides 'Flashing Light'
Maiden Pink (UK and USA)

Height: 15-23cm (6-9in)   Spread: 15cm (6in)
A beautiful rock-garden plant for crevices and between natural paving slabs. From mid-summer to autumn it reveals bright crimson flowers. Other forms include 'Wisley Variety' (carmine-red) and 'Brilliant' (bright rose-pink).

Diascia x 'Ruby Field'
Height: 25-30cm (10-12in)   Spread: 30-38cm (12-15in)
A spreading and somewhat mat-forming hardy rock garden plant with small toothed leaves and warm glowing pink flowers during much of summer.

Phlox douglasii 'Eva'
Height: 5-10cm (2-4in)   Spread: 30-45cm (1-1½ft)
A low-growing shrubby rock-garden plant forming a mat of mid-green leaves and small pink flowers during early summer.

Saxifraga aizoon rosea
(Saxifraga paniculata rosea)

Height: 15-20cm (6-8in)   Spread: 15-25cm (6-10in)
A beautiful euaizoonia saxifraga with wide lance-shaped silver-green leaves and sprays of deep pink early summer flowers. It is also suitable for growing in containers.

Sempervivum arachnoideum
Cobweb Houseleek (UK)
Cobweb Houseleek · Spiderweb Houseleek (USA)

Height: 10cm (4in)   Spread: 23-30cm (9-12in)
A widely-grown succulent plant with rosettes of green leaves, often flushed with red, and bright red, 18mm (¾in) wide flowers during mid-summer.

Phlox subulata
Moss Phlox (UK)
Moss Pink · Moss Phlox · Mountain Phlox (USA)

Height: 5-10cm (2-4in)   Spread: 30-45cm (1-1½ft)
A beautiful sub-shrub forming a mat of mid-green, narrow leaves with pink or purple flowers in spring. Forms to look for include 'Alexander's Surprise' (salmon-pink), 'Scarlet Flame' (brilliant scarlet), 'Star Glow' (bright red) and 'Temiscaming' (brilliant magenta-red).

Thymus drucei is the parent of several unusual and exciting forms, such as 'Lanuginosa' with greyish woolly leaves and lilac flowers, and 'Silver Queen' with silver and green variegated leaves.

CHAPTER THREE

CONTAINER GARDENING

One of the joys of gardening in containers is that the plants otherwise denied to the gardener through lack of space can still be enjoyed. Even small town gardens with just a concreted paved area still offer the opportunity of growing roses, one of the most popular and best known of all garden plants. Miniature roses retain the charm of their big brothers, and have the benefit of near thornless stems that make cultivation very easy — and painless. Roses need deep window-boxes or troughs with a good reservoir of loam-based compost. They must be kept well-watered in summer. Miniature roses, like their larger relatives, produce flowers on shoots developed the same year, so the bushes need pruning early in the year when they are still dormant, or just as growth is starting. In cold areas, leave pruning until late spring or the newly-produced shoots induced by the action of early pruning will be damaged by late frost. In the section *Other plants to consider* on page 67 at the end of this chapter there is a list of suitable miniature rose varieties that have pink or red flowers.

The Ivy-leaved Geranium (*Pelargonium peltatum*) is spectacular in a hanging basket, but it can also be used effectively in a wall basket, which is essentially a hanging basket cut vertically in half. Wall baskets are easily hooked onto a vertical surface, at eye-height or slightly higher. Remember that such containers need frequent watering in summer and that excess water may run down the wall. On brick walls this is often not a problem, but plants positioned on a colour-washed wall can create stains. This can be prevented by lining the basket with a polythene bag and ensuring that the drainage holes that have to be pierced in its base are towards the front. As well as the trailing Ivy-leaved Geranium, with long stems up to 90cm (3ft) long, other plants can be used.

When selecting the range of plants to be used in the garden, give some thought to the background against which they will be displayed. Red-flowered plants look vibrant and striking against a white wall; scarlet flowers look particularly dramatic. Pink-flowered container plants look superb set against a grey wall, and in such a position plants with deep red flowers can also be used to effect.

Left: **Cascade type pelargoniums** *are superb in window-boxes and hanging-baskets. They create a profusion of red flowers that fill the container with stunning, vibrant colour*

Above: **Amaranthus caudatus** *This half-hardy annual is worthy of a place in any garden. The long tassels of crimson flowers are borne from mid-summer to autumn. It looks superb when planted in large containers.*

Amaranthus caudatus

Love-lies-bleeding (UK)
Love-lies-bleeding · Tassel Flower (USA)

A beautiful tropical half-hardy annual with large light green leaves and drooping 38-45cm (15-18in) long tassels of crimson flowers from mid-summer to autumn. In late summer and autumn the leaves and stems take on a bronze or crimson appearance. It is ideal for mixed borders and beds of annuals, or for planting in large containers such as tubs.
Height: 90cm-1.2m (3-4ft)
Spread: 38-45cm (15-18in)
Cultivation: Fertile, moisture-retentive and well-cultivated soil in a sunny position assures success. When grown in containers, use loam-based compost.
Propagation: During mid-spring, sow seeds 3mm (⅛in) deep in loam-based compost in 15°C/59°F. When they are large enough to handle, prick off the seedlings into pots or boxes of loam-based compost and place them in a cold frame to harden off. Plant them out in the garden or in containers when all risk of frost has passed. When grown in a bed of annuals, the seeds can be sown *in situ* during late spring. Thin the seedlings to 38-45cm (15-18in) apart when big enough to handle.

Camellia japonica

Of all tub-grown plants this hardy evergreen shrub is one of the most spectacular. The dark green, leathery leaves taper to a point, while the 7.5-15cm (3-6in) wide flowers appear from late winter to late spring, in a colour range from white to pink, red and purple. At one time this plant was thought to be quite tender, but it has since proved to be relatively hardy, although the flowers are easily damaged by early-morning sun glancing on those covered with a layer of frost.
Height: 1.8-2.4m (6-8ft) in tubs

Camellia japonica has lovely red and pink forms, including 'Donation' (large semi-double clear pink), 'Adolph Audusson' (blood-red with yellow stamens) and 'Laura Walker' (semi-double and bright red).

Above: **Camellia japonica** *This distinctive shrub with early season flowers is a delight on a sheltered patio or terrace. It also does well in the surrounds of a block of flats where the limited size of the gardens available to the occupants has to be used with great care.*

Height: 15-23cm (6-9in)
Spread: 10-15cm (4-6in)
Cultivation: Light, well-drained but moisture-retentive soil suits it. When grown in the garden, the bulbs should be set in position, 13-15cm (5-6in) deep, in autumn. This is usually best done after summer-flowering plants have been removed. Set the bulbs about 15cm (6in) apart. Leave them in position until after they flower, then lift and replant them in an out-of-the-way position where they can be left undisturbed to bloom during the following and successive years in a naturalized display.

When grown in containers, use loam-based compost, setting the bulbs 13-15cm (5-6in) deep and the same distance apart. Plant the bulbs during autumn. When grown in small-area containers take care to ensure that the compost does not become alternately waterlogged and then frozen for long periods during winter. After flowering, replant among shrubs.
Propagation: Buy fresh, healthy bulbs each year for replanting.

Spread: 1.5-1.8m (5-6ft) in tubs
Cultivation: Camellias in containers need to be planted in large tubs. Use a well-drained compost, such as three parts peat, two of loam and one of sharp sand. Ensure the base of the tub is pierced with several holes and a thick layer of coarse drainage material placed over them. Position the tub out of cold winds and direct early morning sunshine. During late spring after flowering cut back any straggly shoots.
Propagation: During mid to late summer, take 7.5-10cm (3-4in) long cuttings, inserting them in pots containing equal parts peat and sharp sand. Keep at 13°C (15°F). When the cuttings are rooted, pot them up into lime-free compost. Then gradually pot up into large pots until the plants can be set in a tub. Although it is normally easier to increase this plant by layering low shoots, this is nearly impossible when it is grown in a tub.

Hyacinthus orientalis

Common Hyacinth · Garden Hyacinth (UK)
Hyacinth · Dutch Hyacinth Common Hyacinth (USA)

Most gardeners and houseplant enthusiasts are familiar with these beautifully-scented bulbs that are equally at home in raised beds, tubs, troughs and window-boxes, as well as in spring-bedding schemes in borders. They can also be induced to flower during winter and early spring indoors, but specially prepared bulbs are needed. The true species is no longer generally grown and it is the larger-flowered Dutch hyacinths that are commonly seen. These have elegant, scented, 10-15cm (4-6in) high spires of wax-like flowers in a wide colour range. Pink and red forms include 'Amsterdam' (salmon-pink), 'Jan Bois' (cerise-pink), 'La Victoire' (red) and 'Pink Pearl' (pink).

Below: **Hyacinthus orientalis**
Many of these bulbs are suitable for growing indoors, while some are ideal for planting in containers on patios and terraces, or for using in formal spring-bedding displays.

Hyacinthus orientalis does well in a large tub, cohabiting with other spring-flowering bulbs. Pink hyacinths mix well in tubs and window-boxes with red species tulips, Grape Hyacinths and yellow crocuses.

CONTAINER GARDENING

Petunia x hybrida

Common Garden Petunia (USA)

A half-hardy perennial best grown as a half-hardy annual, and used in containers as well as for bedding schemes in the garden. The large trumpet-shaped flowers appear from mid to late summer and often into autumn, and are available in a wide colour range. The *Single Multiflora* types (height 15-23cm/6-9in) include 'Gypsy' (coral salmon-red) and 'Resisto' (rose-pink). *Single Grandiflora* types (height 23-30cm/9-12in) include 'Pink Cascade' (pink, and ideal for hanging-baskets) and 'Sparkler' (large bright scarlet).

Cultivation: Light, well-drained and moderately-rich compost is best for containers. Excessively rich compost encourages lush growth at the expense of flowers.

Propagation: During late winter and early spring, sow seeds lightly and thinly in loam-based compost in 15°C (59°F). After germination, and when large enough to handle, prick off the seedlings into boxes or pots of loam-based compost. Slowly harden off the plants and set them in containers or the garden when all risk of frost has passed.

Top: **Petunia x hybrida**
The large trumpet-shaped heads of this Argentinean half-hardy annual are a delight in all types of containers, from window-boxes and troughs to hanging-baskets.

Above: **Zinnia elegans**
Large-flowered and tall varieties can be grown in big tubs, but it is the small types that are better for troughs and window-boxes. Also, these smaller types are easier to blend with other container plants.

Left: **Salvia splendens**
'Flarepath' *The bright scarlet flower spikes of this half-hardy annual contrast well with its dark foliage. It is ideal for summer-bedding schemes, as well as for planting in containers and window-boxes.*

Salvia splendens

Scarlet Sage (UK)
Scarlet Salvia (USA)

A well-known Mexican half-hardy perennial usually grown as a half-hardy annual for use in summer-bedding schemes and containers, from tubs to window-boxes. It is a plant with bright-green toothed-edged foliage and 4-5cm (1½-2in) long scarlet flowers which are themselves surrounded by scarlet bracts. Flowering is over a long period, from mid-summer to the frosts of autumn. Forms include white, scarlet, purple and salmon flowers, such as 'Flarepath' (bright scarlet), 'Blaze of Fire' (bright scarlet) and 'Carabiniere' (intense scarlet).

Height: 30-38cm (12-15in)
Spread: 30-38cm (12-15in)

The name **petunia** is derived from the Brazilian *petun*, meaning tobacco, and refers to the petunia's affinity with the tobacco plant. Both belong to the same plant family, the Solanaceae.

Salvia splendens, with its scarlet flowers, is an obvious colour-contrasting candidate for summer bedding schemes. Whites, light blues and silver-leaved plants are excellent companions.

Cultivation: Ordinary well-drained garden soil and a sunny position assure success. Nipping out the tips of the growing shoots when the plants are 7.5cm (3in) high encourages bushiness.

Propagation: During late winter and early spring sow seeds 6mm (¼in) deep in loam-based compost at 20°C (68°F). When they are large enough to handle, prick out the seedlings into boxes of loam-based compost and slowly harden off in a cold frame. Plant out into the garden after all risk of frost has passed.

Zinnia elegans

Youth and Age (UK)
Common Zinnia · Youth-and-old-Age (USA)

This well known half-hardy Mexican annual normally grows to 60-75cm (2-2½ft). It is therefore the lower growing types, at 15-38cm (6-15in) high, that are better for troughs and window-boxes. The taller types can also be grown, but are best reserved for large tubs, and then in a massed display. The lower forms are often in mixed colours as well as single types. Those in pink and red include 'Pink Buttons' (salmon-pink) and 'Red Riding Hood' (scarlet).

Cultivation: Well-drained loam-based compost is needed, and to ensure that the relatively small quantities of soil in troughs and window-boxes do not dry out during summer, water your zinnias regularly. A sunny and sheltered position suits them, and pinching out the tips of young plants encourages bushiness. Also, remove dead flowers to encourage the development of further ones.

Propagation: During early spring sow seeds 6mm (¼in) deep in trays of loam-based compost, kept at 15°C (59°F). When they are large enough to handle, prick out the seedlings into boxes or pots and slowly harden them off in a cold frame. Plant them out into containers as soon as all risk of frost has passed.

Further plants to consider

Begonia semperflorens

Height: 15-23cm (6-9in)   Spread: 15-23cm (6-9in)
This well-known summer-bedding begonia is really a greenhouse perennial, but is usually grown as a half-hardy annual. It can also be used in containers on patios and terraces. It is a bushy, much-branched plant with glossy bright-green leaves and pink, red and white flowers from mid to late summer, and often into autumn. Red and pink forms include 'Sheila' (vivid orange-scarlet), 'Rosanova' (cerise pink), 'Pink Avalanche' (pink, and ideal for window-boxes, hanging baskets and tubs), 'Pandy' (blood red), 'Carmine (rose-pink) and 'Indian Maid' (deep scarlet).

Impatiens: Hybrid Varieties

These abundantly flowering half-hardy perennials are often treated as half-hardy annuals for bedding schemes and for growing in containers. A single-colour form, 'Blitz' (15cm/6in) has orange-scarlet flowers and is a good choice for planting in tubs and window boxes, while 'Rosette' (15cm/65in) has a mixture of colours including scarlet, rose, salmon, pink and white.

Mimulus 'Malibu'

Height: 10-15cm (4-6in)   Spread: 15cm (6in)
This is one of the most outstanding forms of this half-hardy annual, with a compact but vigorous habit and very deep orange flowers during summer. It is ideal for hanging baskets as well as troughs and window-boxes.

Pelargonium peltatum

Ivy-leaved Geranium (UK)
Ivy Geranium · Hanging Geranium (USA)

Trailing stems up to 90cm (3ft) long.
A superb pelargonium for hanging baskets or the fronts of window-boxes or troughs. Red and pink forms include 'Madame Crouse' (double, bright pink), 'Mexican Beauty' (single, crimson), 'Galilee' (double, rose), 'Lilac Gem' (double, pale pink), 'Mrs W.A.R. Clifton' (double, scarlet), 'Sir Percy Blakeney' (double, rich crimson-scarlet) and 'Ville de Paris' (deep salmon to pink).

Roses — Miniature Types

These are just like normal roses, but a great deal smaller. The almost thornless branches bear double or semi-double flowers 18-40mm (¾-1½in) wide in clusters during mid-summer. Many continue to flower intermittently for much of summer. These miniatures are suitable for deep window-boxes or troughs. Even within this group there is a wide range of sizes, from those at 23cm (9in) to types at 30-38cm (12-15in). The colour range is wide and includes white, yellow, orange and purple. Pink and red forms include 'Cinderella' (15-23cm/6-9in: double and shell-pink, merging to white at the edges), 'Darling Flame' (30-38cm/12-15in: fragrant, and bright orange-red), 'Maid Marion' (20-25cm/8-10in: deep red), 'New Penny' (20cm/8in: semi-double salmon-pink and orange), 'Peria de Monserrat' (30-38cm/12-15in: double and rose-pink) and 'Rouletti' (23-30cm/9-12in: double and rose-pink).

Zinnias are named after the German botanist Johann Gotfried Zinn (1727-1759). *Zinnia elegans*, originally native to Mexico, comes in a wide colour range, including striking red and pink forms.

CHAPTER FOUR

WALL AND TRELLIS FILLERS

Red has often been thought of as the colour of love and perhaps this is confirmed by the 17th Century English poet Milton's line "Celestial rosy-red, love's proper hue". Two hundred years later, in Victorian England, a red rose given by a gentleman to a lady expressed love, though since ancient times it has also been a symbol of silence, giving rise to the Latin phrase *sub rosa*, meaning confidentiality. Even today, a red rose is taken to mean silent love. It is therefore not surprising that red-flowering plants climbing over a lover's arbour, perhaps of trelliswork, should harmonize and present a powerful and satisfying picture.

The largest-flowered and perhaps best known of all clematis happily creates a spectacular summer picture. This is 'Nelly Moser', with mauve-pink flowers decorated with carmine bars. It is truly one of the gems of the flower garden. Created by the French plant breeder Jean Jacques Moser in 1897, it has given pleasure ever since. However, if you like your reds bright and repeat-flowering over a long period, choose *Clematis* 'Ville de Lyon' instead. It produces a burst of bright carmine-red flowers, deeper at their edges and with golden stems, first in early summer and then, with a brief interval, through to late summer and even into autumn.

The ever-reliable Mountain Clematis, *Clematis montana*, has a rose-pink form, 'Rubens'. This variety has the bonus of a slight vanilla scent. The variety 'Elizabeth' also has a slight scent, and large soft pink flowers.

In autumn, the cold weather and frosts heralding the onset of winter soon bring colour to several spectacular climbers blessed with exceptionally attractive leaves. There are five or six excellent wall climbers in the Virginia Creeper family, and some are vigorous enough to clothe the entire wall of a mansion. The Chinese Virginia Creeper, however, is more restrained and better suited to most gardens. Its dark green leaves with white and pink veins are enhanced in autumn when the green turns brilliant red.

Heights and spreads given for the plants in this chapter should only be taken as guides; if more space is available in one direction, the plant will adapt its growth accordingly.

Left: **Clematis 'Ville de Lyon'**, *a large-flowered clematis, creates a screen of colour from mid-summer to late autumn, with bright carmine-red heads.*

WALL AND TRELLIS FILLERS

Abutilon megapotamicum

Trailing Abutilon (USA)

A distinctive, somewhat tender wall shrub with slender stems bearing three-lobed, slender-pointed bright green leaves. During early to late summer, it reveals pendulous, bell-shaped, red and yellow flowers.

Height: 1.5-1.8m (5-6ft)
Spread: 1.8-2.4m (6-8ft)
Cultivation: Good, well-drained garden soil in a sheltered and sunny position is essential. It is not hardy outside in all areas. In cold areas it is best grown in a greenhouse. This plant does not need regular pruning.

A greenhouse border abutilon, somewhat similar to *A. megapotamicum*, is *A. x milleri*. It is a garden hybrid between *A. megapotamicum* and *A. pictum*. In a greenhouse border it rises to 1.8m (6ft) high and 2.4 (8ft) wide, although in a large pot it reaches only about half this size. It is a plant which is well worth growing in a pot in a conservatory. It has the same slender habit as *A. megapotamicum*, with 4cm (1½in) long yellow flowers striped red from late spring to late autumn. Another abutilon for a greenhouse border is *A. x hybridum* 'Ashford Red', with similar growth measurements as *A. x milleri* when grown in a greenhouse border or in a pot. The mid-green three to five-lobed leaves present a perfect foil for the 4cm (1½in) long pendant salmon-red flowers borne from late spring to late summer.

Propagation: During mid-summer take 7.5-10cm (3-4in) long half-ripe cuttings. Insert in pots containing equal parts peat and sharp sand and keep at 15°C (58°F). When the plants are rooted, pot them up into loam-based compost.

Right: **Abutilon megapotamicum**
This fairly tender wall shrub soon attracts attention with its red and yellow flowers, borne from early to late summer. A sunny position against a wall is essential.

Abutilon megapotamicum is an adaptable plant. Its slender stems allow it to be trained to suit many positions — in corners, under windows or between large windows. It needs wire for support.

Above: **Camellia x williamsii 'Donation'** *This lovely shrub thrives in an acid soil and a sheltered position, producing a wealth of semi-double orchid-pink flowers from late winter to spring. Avoid places where the early-morning sun will shine on frost-covered flowers.*

Camellia x williamsii

This well-known hardy evergreen shrub is a hybrid between *Camellia japonica*, the Common Camellia, and *Camellia salvenensis*, the Salwin River Camellia from Western China. The flowers, which appear even on small plants, are either single or semi-double and range from white and pink to rose-purple, all displaying distinctive yellow stamens. They are 5-7.5cm (2-3in) wide and appear from early winter to spring. Pink forms include 'Citation' (semi-double and pale pink), 'Coppelia' (single and carmine-rose), 'Donation' (semi-double and silvery-pink), 'J.C. Williams' (single and blush-pink), 'November Pink' (single, early and bright pink) and 'St. Ewe' (single, funnel-shaped and rose-pink).
Height: 1.8-2.4m (6-8ft)
Spread: 1.2-1.8m (4-6ft)

Cultivation: Fertile, light, acid moisture-retentive soil and a position in sun or partial shade suit this beautiful shrub. Light shade from trees is ideal, giving protection from frost and strong sun in the early morning. A south-facing position should be avoided because these plants need a cool root-run. No pruning is needed, except in the initial shaping of the shrub and the annual removal of misplaced and straggling shoots.
Propagation: During mid-summer, take 7.5-10cm (3-4in) long cuttings and insert them in pots containing equal parts peat and sharp sand, kept at 13°C (55°F). Pot up the rooted cuttings into an acid loam-based compost and slowly acclimatize them to a lower temperature. Alternatively, layer low-growing shoots in early autumn, although it takes about 18 months to produce roots.

Camellia japonica, the Common Camellia, is a splendid shrub with some beautiful red varieties, such as 'Chandleri' (semi-double), 'Donckelarii' (semi-double flowers) and 'Mathotiana' (double).

Above: **Cotoneaster horizontalis** *A reliable shrub that brings colour to any garden in autumn with its beautiful red berries. It is excellent for planting against walls, on banks or as ground-cover.*

Parthenocissus tricuspidata

(Vitis inconstans)
Boston Ivy (UK)
Boston Ivy · Japanese Ivy (USA)

This is a hardy and vigorous self-clinging deciduous climber from China, Japan, Korea and Taiwan. The shape of the leaves is variable, but usually toothed and trifoliate in young leaves and three-lobed in older ones. In autumn they turn a gloriously rich crimson and scarlet. The form 'Veitchii' (previously known as *Ampelopsis veitchii*) bears small leaves tinged purple when young.
Height: 7.5-15m (20-50ft)
Spread: 4.5-7.5m (15-25ft)
Cultivation: Fertile soil and a large wall or tree up which it can climb are the essential elements for success with this beautiful and popular climber; given these, it flourishes with little or no assistance.
Propagation: During late summer take 10-13cm (4-5in) long cuttings. Insert them in sandy compost and keep at 13°C (55°F). Pot up when rooted. Alternatively, long shoots can be layered in late autumn.

Cotoneaster horizontalis

Herringbone Cotoneaster ·
Fishbone Cotoneaster (UK)
Rock Cotoneaster (USA)

This popular semi-evergreen or deciduous hardy shrub has small, dark glossy green leaves borne on stiff frameworks of branches that spread out in a herringbone fashion. The 8-12mm (⅓-½in) wide pink flowers appear in mid-summer and are followed in autumn by round red berries borne in profusion along the branches. This is an adaptable shrub with many roles in the garden, from covering banks, where it will rise to 60cm (2ft) with a spread up to 1.8m (6ft), to sprawling over low walls or planting against a wall, where it will grow to 1.8-2.4m (6-8ft) tall with a spread of 1.5-2.1m (5-7ft). It is an ideal shrub for east and north-facing walls.
Cultivation: Any good garden soil and a sunny position suit it, although it is hardy enough for a cold wall.
Propagation: Although it can be increased by seeds sown in autumn or early winter in pots of loam-based compost, placed in a cold frame or a sheltered position in a corner of the garden, this method takes a long time to produce sizeable plants. As an alternative, take heel cuttings 7.5-10cm (3-4in) long in late summer and insert them in pots of equal parts peat and sand, placed in a cold frame. Plant out the cuttings in a nursery bed when they are rooted and established. A further method is to layer low-growing shoots in late autumn or early winter.

Robinia hispida

Rose Acacia (UK)
Moss Locust · Rose Acacia ·
Bristly Locust · Mossy Locust (USA)

This is an open, rather gaunt hardy deciduous shrub from South-east North America, ideal for growing against a south or west-facing wall. The dark green leaves, up to 25cm (10in) long, are formed of seven to thirteen leaflets each 4-6.5cm (1½-2½in) long. The distinctive pea-like rose-pink flowers are about 3cm (1¼in) long and borne in drooping bunches of five to ten flowers, in early to mid-summer.
Height: 1.8-2.4m (6-8ft)
Spread: 2.1-2.7m (7-9ft)
Cultivation: Any well-drained moderately-rich soil in a sunny position suits a robinia. Avoid excessively rich soil. No regular pruning is needed.

Cotoneaster horizontalis planted against a high wall at the back of a border provides a useful foil for many shrubs, including azaleas. When grown as ground-cover in a border, it merges with other shrubs, especially grey-leaved ones.

Propagation: It is best raised by grafting onto its relative *Robinia pseudoacacia*, although suckers can be detached from the bases of non-grafted plants.

Above: **Parthenocissus tricuspidata**
This hardy deciduous climber produces a generous covering of rich crimson and scarlet leaves in autumn. The only drawback is that it needs a large wall up which to climb. Alternatively, it is at home climbing a large, old tree that would be enhanced by a dash of colour and glamour in autumn.

Right: **Robinia hispida**
The pea-like rose-pink flowers of this early-summer-flowering wall shrub are especially appealing against an old brick wall. A sunny position is essential for success.

Parthenocissus henryana, the Chinese Virginia Creeper, is best suited to a small garden, and it requires a sheltered position. The leaves, formed of three or five leaflets, turn shades of red in autumn.

Robinia hispida was first seen and collected by an Englishman, Mark Catesby, in the foothills of the Appalachian Mountains in 1714. Before he was able to collect seeds the region was burnt by Indians.

WALL AND TRELLIS FILLERS

Right: **Tropaeolum speciosum**
Bright scarlet flowers appear on the scrambling stems during summer, with a backcloth provided by mid-green six-lobed leaves. The plant is seen at its best when it is growing through and over other shrubs.

Tropaeolum majus

Nasturtium · Great Indian Cress (UK)

A well-known and widely-grown climbing and trailing hardy annual from South America, ideal for covering fences, trelliswork and for scrambling over banks. The highly distinctive smooth and mid-green leaves are circular, and the early to late summer 5cm (2in) wide orange or yellow flowers are faintly scented. Also, the leaves have a strong, pungent smell. The colour range has been extended to include red, pink and maroon flowers.
Height: 1.7-2.4m (6-8ft) climbing type
Spread: 60cm-1.2m (2-4ft) climbing type
Cultivation: This is an ideal plant for poor soils and a sunny position. If the soil is rich, the growth of the plants is excessive and at the expense of the flowers. Initially, the young plants need twiggy sticks up which to climb, but once established on a trellis or wire framework, they need no extra support.
Propagation: During spring, seeds can be sown 18mm (¾in) deep where the plants are to flower. If the seedlings are crowded, thin them out to 10-15cm (4-6in) apart. However, for early-flowering plants, especially those for hanging baskets, sow seeds in early spring in trays of loam-based seed compost at 13°C (55°F). When they are large enough to handle, put the seedlings singly in 7.5cm (3in) pots and slowly harden them off in a cold frame until they can be planted outside during late spring or early summer when they are growing strongly.

Left: **Tropaeolum majus**
The original form of this hardy trailing and climbing annual is yellow and orange, but seedsmen have extended the colour range to include red, pink and maroon. It is an ideal climber for poor soil.

Tropaeolum speciosum

Flame Creeper · Flame Nasturtium · Scotch Flame Flower

An exotic-looking Chilean deciduous perennial climber, the Flame Creeper has a creeping rhizome-producing rootstock that dies down to soil-level in autumn. It has a sprawling growth habit, with downy and hairy stems bearing six-lobed mid-green leaves, which have downy undersides. During

Tropaeolum majus has long been used by cooks as well as gardeners. The flowers and young leaves can be added to salads, and have a warm taste not unlike that of common cress.

mid-summer to autumn it reveals 4cm (1½in) wide long-stemmed trumpet-like scarlet flowers formed of five rounded and waved petals.

Height: 3-4.5m (10-15ft)

Spread: 75cm-1m (2½-3½ft)

Cultivation: Acid or neutral soil enriched with leafmould and peat suits this plant. It does best when planted in association with a shrub through which its stems can clamber. The flowers are then able to reach the light, while the roots remain cool.

Propagation: It is easily increased by lifting and dividing the roots in early spring, setting them 15-20cm (6-8in) deep. Take care not to damage the fleshy roots. It can also be increased by sowing seeds in a cold frame in spring, but it is difficult to establish.

Further plants to consider

Aklebia quinta
Five-leaf Akebia · Chocolate Vine (USA)

Height: 1.5-2.4m (5-8ft) Spread: 1.2-1.5m (4-5ft)
A sprawling and lax semi-evergreen climber with leaves formed of five leaflets. The fragrant red-purple flowers appear in spring.

Berberidopsis corallina
Coral Plant (UK)

Height: 4.5m (15ft) Spread: 2.4-3.5m (8-12ft)
A distinctive evergreen climber well suited to a shaded and sheltered wall. During mid to late summer, it bears clusters of deep coral-crimson flowers.

Campsis radicans
Trumpet Vine (UK)
Cow-itch · Trumper Honeysuckle (USA)

A superb self-clinging hardy deciduous climber with light green leaves formed of seven to eleven leaflets. During late summer, it displays rich scarlet and orange trumpet-shaped flowers.

Clematis montana 'Rubens'
Mountain Clematis (UK)

Height: 7.5-10.5m 625-35ft) Spread: 4.5-6m (15-20ft)
A beautiful vigorous deciduous climber with bronze-green leaves and pale pink flowers.

Clematis — Large-flowered

Several of these magnificent shrubs have red and pink forms, including 'Ernest Markham' (petunia-red), 'Hagley Hybrid' (shell-pink), 'Nelly Moser' (mauve-pink) with a carmine bar) and 'Ville de Lyon' (bright carmine-red).

Lapageria rosea
Chilean Bell Flower (UK)   Chile-bells · Copihue (USA)

Height: 3-4.5m (10-15ft) Spread: 1.8-2.4m (6-8ft)
A semi-hardy, tender, evergreen climber that needs a sheltered and relatively frost free position. From mid-summer to autumn, it displays rose-crimson bell-shaped flowers, singly or in clusters.

Parthenocissus quinquefolia
(Vitis quinquefolia · Vitis hederacea)
True Virginia Creeper · Virginia Creeper (UK)
American Ivy · Five-leaved Ivy · Virginia Creeper (USA)

Height: 12-18m (40-60ft) Spread: 6-10.5m (20-35ft)
A vigorous and spreading hardy deciduous climber with matt-green leaves, formed of three or five leaflets, which turn brilliant scarlet and orange in autumn.

Tropaeolum speciosum is useful for growing through shrubs, but it can also be planted in conjunction with a climber, such as the variegated small-leaved ivy *Hedera helix* 'Goldheart'.

CHAPTER FIVE

TREES AND SHRUBS

A canopy of pink flowers trailing over daffodils is a sure sign spring has finally rid herself of the shackles of winter. One of the finest of all pink-flowering trees and shrubs is the tree *Prunus subhirtella* 'Pendula'. Another is the early summer-flowering shrub *Kolkwitzia amabilis*; it is aptly called the Beauty Bush. It was introduced into cultivation by the great Scottish plant-hunter Ernest Henry Wilson (1876-1930). He made four journeys to China, Japan and Taiwan (Formosa) and returned from Western China in 1901 with specimens of the Beauty Bush for the world-famous Veitch nursery in Edinburgh, Scotland. It has been an outstanding pink-flowered shrub ever since.

There is a wealth of trees and shrubs producing reds and scarlets in their leaves during autumn, including many members of the Maple family, a group seen at their best in the New England region of North America during fall. Other well-known examples are *Cercidiphyllum japonicum*, the Katsura Tree from Japan; *Liquidambar styraciflua*, the North American Sweet Gum, and *Parrotia persica*, from Iran and the Caucasus. The Sweet Gum has lobed, palm-like, brilliant orange and scarlet autumn leaves. The wide-spreading branches of *Parrotia persica* bear mid-green leaves which turn rich crimson, amber and gold in autumn. A grove of these trees as a seasonal focal point in a large garden is stunning. The Paperbark Maple, *Acer griseum*, is an equal success in autumn with its red and crimson trifoliate leaves which last through to winter. Then, the bare branches fully reveal the light orange-brown underbark. When the ground is covered with snow, the contrast highlights the colourful bark even more. It is an ideal tree for a small garden, reaching only 4.5m (15ft) after twenty or so years.

Many trees and shrubs bear rich red berries in autumn and often through much of winter; the best known of these belong to the Malus and Sorbus groups. Good malus forms include 'Katherine', with bright red berries flushed red and 'Red Sentinel', with large cardinal-red berries that continue through to early spring.

The heights and spreads given for plants in this chapter are those they should reach twenty years after planting in good soil.

Left: Azaleas *and* rhododendrons *are superb for creating colour in spring and summer. Azaleas are especially rich in pastel shades.*

Acer palmatum 'Dissectum Atropurpureum'

This hardy and reliable deciduous shrub is a delight in any garden, producing a dome-like canopy of finely-cut bronze-red leaves throughout summer.

Height: 1.2-1.5m (4-5ft)
Spread: 2.1-2.7m (7-9ft)
Cultivation: Well-drained but moisture-retentive cool soil in full sun or light shade suits this shrub. A sheltered position is also useful.
Propagation: It is usually grafted, so its propagation is best left to expert nurserymen.

Left: **Acer palmatum 'Dissectum Atropurpureum'**
When set amid a light green ground-cover plant, this hardy deciduous shrub is superb. It looks just as good planted in the well-manicured lawn of a formal garden.

Below: **Azalea 'Kirin'**
This hardy evergreen azalea, with its magnificent display of deep rose flowers in spring, is ideal for a woodland setting in light shade. Acid soil is essential.

Acer palmatum 'Dissectum' is a similarly shaped and sized form, but with finely-cut light green leaves. In a large garden, plant it to contrast with the bronze-red form, but don't crowd them together.

Azalea 'Kirin'

This is one of the hardy evergreen Kurume azaleas, with a relatively low and spreading habit. In spring it is covered with masses of deep rose flowers. Other superb Kurume types include 'Addy Wery' (vermilion-red), 'Benigirl' (bright crimson), 'Blaauw's Pink' (salmon-pink), 'Hinodegiri' (bright crimson), 'Hinomayo' (clear pink) and 'Rosebud' (rose-pink).

Height: 90cm-1.2m (3-4ft)
Spread: 1.2-1.5m (4-5ft)
Cultivation: Well-drained light acid soil in partial shade and a sheltered position suit it best. Keep the soil well mulched. This azalea grows especially well in a lightly-shaded woodland setting.
Propagation: It can be increased by cuttings, but it is easier for home gardeners to propagate it by layering low-growing shoots in spring. Rooting of these shoots may take up to two years.

Right: **Crataegus laevigata 'Rosea Flore Plena'**
This superb form of this deciduous tree produces double pink flowers in spring that completely cover the attractive foliage.

Crataegus laevigata

(Crataegus oxyacantha)
Hawthorn · May (UK)
English Hawthorn · Quick-set Thorn · White Thorn (USA)

This well-known European native deciduous tree has rounded, shallowly three or five-lobed, mid-green leaves. During late spring and early summer, it reveals 5-7.5cm (2-3in) wide, highly scented, white flowers. But many forms of crataegus create pink or red displays, such as 'Paul's Scarlet' (double and scarlet), 'Rosea' (single and pink) and 'Rosea Flore Plena' (double and pink). *Crataegus monogyna*, the Common May, May or Quick, known in North America as the English Hawthorn, is a densely-branched and thorny tree often used for hedging and bears heavily-scented white flowers in early summer. In contrast, *C. m.* 'Pendula Rosea' is a pink-flowered form with pendulous and graceful branches. Many crataegus species are known for their attractive fruits. *Crataegus x grignonensis*, a small hybrid, is a late flowering form with long-lasting, large, bright-red fruits. It also has the bonus of leaves that remain green up until winter. *Crataegus x lavallei*, also known as *C. x carrierei*, is densely branched with orange-red haws that persist throughout winter. During early summer it reveals large clusters of white flowers. *Crataegus x prunifolia* is another hybrid, with spiny branches and a compact head. The early summer white flowers are followed in autumn by large red fruits that persist well into winter.

Height: 4.5-6m (15-20ft)
Spread: 4.5-5.4m (15-18ft)
Cultivation: Any good garden soil and a position in an open and sunny position suit this tree. No regular pruning is needed, other than training the plant during its formative years.
Propagation: Named forms are budded or grafted, and this is best left to specialist nurserymen.

Crataegus laevigata does well as a specimen tree in a lawn or in a mixed border, where it creates a blanket background of colour in spring. Its wide-spreading nature makes it suitable for deep borders.

TREES AND SHRUBS

Deutzia x elegantissima 'Fasciculata'

A widely-grown hardy hybrid deciduous shrub with an upright and busy growth habit. The matt-green, slender-pointed, lance-shaped leaves provide an attractive foil for the sweetly-scented, star-shaped, bright rose-pink, 5-7.5cm (2-3in) wide flowers, borne on arching branches in late spring and early summer.

Height: 1.2-1.5m (4-5ft)

Spread: 1.2-1.5m (4-5ft)

Cultivation: Ordinary well-drained garden soil in full sun or light shade suits it well. Flower colours tend not to fade rapidly when a deutzia is positioned in light shade During summer, after flowering, cut out old flowered stems to soil-level. This encourages the development of fresh shoots from the shrub's base.

Propagation: Although half-ripe 7.5-10cm (3-4in) long cuttings can be taken in mid-summer and inserted in equal parts peat and sharp sand, it is easier for the home gardener to take 25-30cm (10-12in) long hardwood cuttings in autumn. Insert them in a trench in a nursery bed. Line the base of the trench with sand.

Embothrium coccineum

Chilean Fire Bush (UK)
Chilean Fire Tree · Chilean Firebush (USA)

This eye-catching ornamental evergreen tree has an upright growth habit, and produces suckers. The leaves, which are scattered along the branches, are leathery, lance-shaped and mid-green. During early to mid-summer, it produces brilliant orange-scarlet flowers, tubular when they first appear. It is not fully hardy in all areas, and in cold places is severely damaged by frosts. The form 'Norquinco Valley' is a hardier type.

Height: 4.5-6m (15-20ft)

Spread: 2.4-3m (8-10ft)

Cultivation: Well-drained but moisture-retentive neutral or acid deep woodland soil suits it best. In most gardens a position facing south or west and against a high wall is perfect. In winter, protect young plants with a covering of straw. No regular pruning is needed, other than initially removing misplaced shoots and later shortening straggly growths after flowering.

Propagation: Although seeds can be sown in spring in loam-based compost at 13°C (55°F), it is far easier for home gardeners to remove sucker growths from around the base of the tree and then pot them up. Plant the young trees in late spring.

Above: **Deutzia x elegantissima 'Fasciculata'** *This hardy deciduous shrub is a delight in late spring and early summer, with its bright rose-pink flowers backed by a foil of matt-green leaves. It is ideal for a small garden.*

Right: **Embothrium coccineum** *This is one of the most spectacular and desirable of all garden trees, although it is really hardy only in milder areas. The superb fiery flowers appear in late spring.*

Top right: **Gaultheria procumbens** *This beautiful carpeting sub-shrub has glorious berries in autumn. This is the plant from which Wintergreen Oil is obtained, a volatile pale-green substance.*

Deutzia scabra, which bears cluster of white flushed pink cup-shaped flowers, was at one time prized in Japan by polishers. Its leaves, with their rigid, star-shaped hairs, could be used as natural rougheners.

Embothrium coccineum does well when set in woodland among other trees and shrubs that give it some protection. It blends well with azaleas and heathers, which create interest at a lower level.

Gaultheria procumbens

Partridge Berry · Winter Green · Checkerberry (UK)
Wintergreen · Checkerberry · Teaberry · Mountain Tea · Ivry-leaves (USA)

A creeping, prostrate, hardy evergreen sub-shrub from North America with shiny dark green slightly-toothed leaves. During late summer, it produces small white or pink bell-shaped flowers, followed in autumn by bright red berries.

Height: 10-15cm (4-6in)
Spread: 75cm-1.2m (2½-4ft)
Cultivation: Acid, moist soil is essential, and a position in the open, or in light shade. Beware of sites where water drips from trees casting shade on the plants.
Propagation: During mid-summer take 5-7.5cm (2-3in) long cuttings with heels and insert them in equal parts peat and sharp sand. Place them in a cold frame. When rooted pot up the plants into small pots of lime-free compost with a high proportion of peat, and place them outside. Preferably, plunge the pots in soil in a nursery bed, so that the compost remains cool and moist.

Gaultheria procumbens was an invaluable plant for early North American settlers. The berries provided winter food for partridge and deer, while the leaves were used as a substitute for tea.

TREES AND SHRUBS

Hibiscus syriacus

(Althaea frutex)
Shrubby Mallow (UK)
Rose-of-sharon · Althaea · Shrub
Althaea (USA)

A native of Syria, this hardy
deciduous shrub provides colour in
mid to late summer and even into
autumn. The 7.5cm (3in) wide
flowers appear in a colour range
from white to pink, purple and red.
Superb pink and red forms include
'Red Heart' (white flowers with
conspicuous red centres),
'Woodbridge' (rose-pink with a
carmine eye) and 'Violaceus
Plenus' (double and wine-red).
Height: 1.8-2.4m (6-8ft)
Spread: 1.2-1.8m (4-6ft)
Cultivation: Well-drained fertile
garden soil and a position in full
sun but sheltered from buffeting
winds suit this lovely shrub.
Regular pruning is not needed, but
long shoots can be cut back
immediately after flowering.
Propagation: During mid-summer,
take 7.5-10cm (3-4in) long heel
cuttings and insert them in pots of
equal parts peat and sharp sand.
Place them in a heated frame at
16°C (61°F) and when the plants
are rooted, pot them up into loam-
based compost and overwinter in a
cold frame. When the plants fill
their pots, transfer them to larger
ones and place outdoors until
autumn, when they can be planted
out into the garden.

Top left: **Hibiscus syriacus
'Woodbridge'**
*This highly distinctive shrub has
large rose-pink flowers with
carmine eyes. A sheltered but
sunny position is essential.*

Kalmia latifolia

Calico Bush · Mountain Laurel (UK)
Mountain Laurel · Calico Bush ·
Ivybush · Spoonwood (USA)

This outstandingly beautiful
evergreen shrub has leathery,
lance-shaped, mid to dark green
leaves. During mid-summer it
displays 7.5-10cm (3-4in) wide
clusters of bowl-shaped, bright pink
flowers. 'Clematine Churchill' is an
attractive form with rich red
flowers. It gains the name
Spoonwood from its use in the
manufacture of household items

Above: **Hibiscus syriacus
'Red Heart'**
*This outstandingly attractive shrub
has white flowers with conspicuous
red centres. It grows best in a
sheltered position in the garden.*

such as spoons and ladles.
Height: 1.8-3m (6-10ft)
Spread: 1.8-2.4m (6-8ft)
Cultivation: Moist, slightly acid
fertile soil in light shade suits it
best. No regular pruning is needed,
other than removing faded flowers.
Propagation: The easiest way for
a home gardener to increase this
plant is by layering low shoots in
late summer. Rooting takes about
a year, when the new plants can
be severed from the parent and
planted in a nursery bed for a year
or so before finally being set out
into the open garden.

Hibiscus rosa-sinensis, a closely-related
greenhouse plant from China, was much favoured by
Chinese ladies. When bruised, the flowers turn black
or purple and were used to dye hair and eyebrows.

Above: **Kalmia latifolia** *This beautiful evergreen mid-summer flowering North American shrub produces clusters of bowl-shaped bright pink flowers. When out of flower, the plant has the appearance of a rhododendron. Position it in acid soil and light shade.*

Below: **Kolkwitzia amabilis 'Pink Beauty'** *This is a real eye-catcher, with its clear pink flowers from late spring to early summer. In winter the brown peeling bark is attractive in the low rays of winter sun.*

Kolkwitzia amabilis

Beauty Bush (UK and USA)

This hardy deciduous shrub from Western China has an upright stance and arching branches displaying dull dark green leaves. The stems have attractive peeling brown bark. During late spring to early summer, it is profusely covered with pink foxglove-like flowers with yellow throats. The best form is 'Pink Cloud' with clear pink flowers.

Height: 1.8-3m (6-10ft)
Spread: 1.5-3m (5-10ft)
Cultivation: Ordinary well-drained garden soil and a position in full sun suit it best. During mid-summer, after the flowers have faded, cut out a few of the older flowering stems at soil-level. This will encourage the development of further shoots.
Propagation: During mid to late summer, take 10-15cm (4-6in) long cuttings from non-flowering shoots. Insert them in pots of equal parts peat and sharp sand and place in a cold frame. When rooted, set the cuttings in a nursery bed for a year. Plant them out into the garden when established.

Kolkwitzia amabilis is ideal for a shrub or mixed border. It looks superb with Foxgloves set in front of it. The thimble-like flowers arranged in long spires form an attractive shape contrast.

Leycesteria formosa

Flowering Nutmeg · Granny's Curls · Pheasant Berry (UK)
Himalaya Honeysuckle (USA)

This handsome and unusual deciduous hardy shrub from the Himalayas has mid-green, heart-shaped leaves and, in late summer, funnel-shaped flower-heads, formed of small white flowers surrounded by highly conspicuous dark claret bracts. These are followed by round, shiny purplish-red berries in autumn.
Height: 1.5-2.1m (5-7ft)
Spread: 1.2-1.5m (4-5ft)
Cultivation: Any well-drained

Above: **Lavatera olbia 'Rosea'**
This shrubby perennial produces a wealth of leaves surmounted by pink-red flowers from mid to late summer, often into early autumn. It grows well in warm, coastal areas.

Lavatera olbia 'Rosea'

Tree Mallow (UK and USA)

This rough-stemmed, vigorous, somewhat tender sub-shrub is native to the Western Mediterranean region. The three to five-lobed soft and woolly grey leaves provide a foil for the large pinkish red flowers borne on short stalks from mid to late summer.
Height: 1.5-2.1m (5-7ft)
Spread: 1.5-1.8m (5-6ft)
Cultivation: Rich well-drained garden soil suits the Tree Mallow, preferably in a warm site in full sun against a wall. Keep the soil moist during summer, and in spring cut back the foliage to soil-level. Leaving the foliage on the plant during winter helps to protect the roots of the plant from severe cold, as well as appearing attractive when covered with frost.
Propagation: During spring, take half-ripe cuttings.

Lavatera arborea is also known as the Tree Mallow, but this is a biennial with an erect growth habit, which has soft mid-green leaves and 5cm (2in) wide pale purple flowers during mid to late summer.

garden soil, preferably in full sun, suits this shrub. It does well in coastal areas. During spring, cut out at soil-level the shoots that bore flowers the previous year.
Propagation: In autumn, take 23-25cm (9-10in) long hardwood cuttings. Insert them in a nursery bed, where they will take about a year to produce roots. They should then be left for a further year.

Below: **Leycesteria formosa**
The eye-catching flowers of this hardy deciduous shrub appear during late summer. In autumn, the flowers are followed by purplish-red berries.

Magnolia liliiflora 'Nigra'

(Magnolia soulangiana 'Nigra')

A spectacular hardy deciduous shrub with rather straggly growth, this magnolia bears mid to dark green leaves up to 20cm (8in) long. During late spring to early summer, it produces handsome 7.5cm (3in) long deep reddish-purple flowers.
Height: 1.7-2.4m (6-8ft)
Spread: 1.5-2.1m (5-7m)
Cultivation: Well-drained loamy garden soil and a sheltered site are essential. During spring, top-dress the soil with well-rotted compost. No regular pruning is needed, other than shaping the

---

Above: **Magnolia liliiflora 'Nigra'**
Few shrubs are as stunningly attractive as this hardy deciduous species with its large, upright, reddish-purple flowers. It is ideal for planting as a specimen in a large lawn.

---

shrub during its formative years.
Propagation: Although cuttings 10cm (4in) long can be taken in mid-summer and inserted in pots containing a sandy compost and kept at 21°C (70°F), it is much easier for a home gardener to layer low shoots in spring. However, these often take up to two years to form roots.

Leycesteria formosa produces its flowers along shoots several feet above soil-level, so lower growing plants such as bergenias and hellebores are best positioned around it.

Magnolias are named in honour of Pierre Magnol, a professor of botany and medicine at Montpelier, Southern France. Most species are said to have aromatic tonic qualities.

TREES AND SHRUBS

Pieris floribunda 'Forest Flame' is ideal if you like
brilliant red early spring foliage. Slowly the leaves
turn pink, then creamy-white and later green. A bonus
is the clusters of drooping white flowers.

Right: **Prunus 'Cheal's Weeping Cherry'**
This mid to late spring-flowering cherry is superb for small gardens. It is correctly known as kiku-shidare Sakura', but in most nursery catalogues it is listed under its English name.

Pieris japonica 'Blush'

An outstanding compact, hardy, evergreen shrub with mid-green leaves, which are coppery when young; and clustered spring heads of pale blush-pink flowers, rose-pink when in bud. The form *P. japonica* 'Christmas Cheer' is especially hardy and develops flowers flushed deep rose at their tips during winter. This Japanese form bears its flowers even on young and small plants. For added interest *P. japonica* 'Variegata' has leaves edged creamy-white, as well as creamy-white flowers flushed pink when young. While the form 'Bert Chandler', raised in Australia, has young salmon-pink foliage before turning green.
Height: 1.8-2.4m (6-8ft)
Spread: 1.5-2.1m (5-7ft)
Cultivation: Moisture-retentive acid soil and light shade suit it well. A sheltered site is also desirable. During spring mulch the plants with well-rotted compost, and in dry summers water the soil.
Propagation: The easiest way for a home gardener to increase it is by layering low shoots in late summer. However rooting is not rapid, often taking up to two years. Alternatively, take 10cm (4in) long cuttings in mid to late summer and insert them in pots of equal parts peat and sharp sand. Place these in a cold frame. In spring, pot up the rooted cuttings into 7.5cm (3in) pots of acid loam-based compost.

Left: **Pieris japonica 'Blush'**
The rose-pink pitcher-like spring flowers never fail to create interest. This shrub has a delicate appearance, like many early-season plants. It needs acid soil.

Prunus — Japanese Cherries

This is the group of cherries so well-known for their beautiful spring and early summer flowers. The origin of most of them is obscure, but some are hybrids, while others are derived from *Prunus speciosa* and *Prunus serrulata spontanea*. Their colours range from pink to white. Pink forms include 'Cheal's Weeping Cherry' (also known as 'Kiku-shidare Sakura' with double pink flowers in early spring); 'Amanogawa' (a small columnar tree, with erect branches bearing fragrant semi-double shell-pink flowers in mid to late spring); 'Kanzan' (a well-known form, eventually making a large tree, which is one of the finest spring-flowering trees when it displays large and showy double purplish-pink flowers in mid-spring); 'Shimidsu Sakura' (a flat-topped, wide-spreading tree with fringed double flowers, pink in bud and opening to white in late spring); and 'Taoyama Zakura' (a small, slow-growing, free-flowering tree with semi-double shell-pink flowers in mid-spring).
Cultivation: Well-drained ordinary garden soil in a sunny position suit Japanese Cherries best. These trees are shallow rooting, so take care not to damage them when cultivating the soil. The wide-spreading types need staking from their earliest years if they are not to fall over later. Pruning is not usually necessary, but if it is required do it in late summer.
Propagation: This involves budding or grafting, so it is best left to expert nurserymen who have the correct rootstocks.

Prunus cerasifera 'Atropurpurea' — often called 'Pissardii' — is known as the Cherry Plum and displays distinctive dark red leaves when young that eventually turn purple.

87

TREES AND SHRUBS

Above: **Prunus sargentii**
This is one of the most attractive cherries, displaying beautiful foliage when unfurling in spring and again in autumn when assuming red and orange tints. The clear pink flowers are borne in spring.

Prunus sargentii

Sargent Cherry (UK)
Sargent Cherry · North Japanese Hill Cherry (USA)

This is one of the most attractive of all cherries, forming a rounded head with bronze-red foliage when young. In autumn, the leaves take on shades of red and orange before falling. It is one of the first trees to show autumn colour. During spring, it produces clusters of clear pink single flowers. The only drawback to this species is that it eventually forms a tree too large for the average small garden.
Height: 7.5-9m (25-30ft)
Spread: 5.4-7.5m (18-25ft)
Cultivation: Ordinary, well-drained garden soil suits the Sargent Cherry. It does well in smoky and polluted areas. Cherries are shallow-rooted, so take care not to damage the roots. No regular pruning is needed, but should the removal of a large branch be necessary, do this in late summer, not during winter.
Propagation: It is increased by budding or grafting, and this is best left to a nurseryman.

Left: **Prunus subhirtella 'Pendula Rosea'**
This stunningly attractive spring-flowering cherry tree forms a distinctive mushroom shape covered with pale pink flowers. It is an excellent choice for small gardens.

Prunus subhirtella 'Pendula'

This lovely hardy deciduous spring-flowering tree creates a weeping mound of pendulous shoots that bear delicate pale pink flowers during spring. There are several other exciting forms, such as *Prunus subhirtella* 'Pendula Rosea', the Weeping Spring Cherry, with pale pink flowers on a mushroom-shaped tree. This is the form often sold by nurseries as *P. subhirtella* 'Pendula', causing confusion between the two species. The form *P. subhirtella* 'Pendula Plena Rosea' is another weeping tree, with semi-double rose-pink spring flowers.
Height: 3-4.5m (10-15ft)
Spread: 3-6m (10-20ft)
Cultivation: Ordinary, well-drained, fertile, neutral soil and a relatively sheltered position suit this tree. Cherry trees are not deeply-rooted, so soil cultivation must be shallow. No regular pruning is needed, but any shaping or large branch removal must be done in late summer, not winter.
Propagation: This is by grafting and budding on to selected stocks and is best left to expert nurserymen.

Ribes sanguineum

Flowering Currant (UK)

This reliable and popular deciduous garden shrub from North America seldom fails to create interest. Its currant-like, mid to deep green, three- to five-lobed leaves provide an attractive foil for the 5-10cm (2-4in) long, deep rose-pink, spring flowers. Several excellent forms are available, including 'Pulborough Scarlet' (rich deep red) and 'King

Prunus subhirtella 'Pendula Rosea' produces a screen of colour right down to soil-level and looks best planted as a specimen tree on a lawn. If crowded with other trees, its distinctive form is lost.

Above: **Ribes sanguineum**
In spring this flowering currant produces a dominant display of deep rose-pink flowers. Several superb forms are available, including a golden-yellow-leaved one that blends with dark leaves.

Edward VII' (deep crimson). The form 'Brocklebankii' is an attractive pink-flowered form, with the bonus of golden-yellow foliage.
Height: 1.7-2.4m (6-8ft)
Spread: 1.5-2.1m (5-7ft)
Cultivation: Any good well-drained soil in full sun or light shade is suitable. Pruning consists of cutting out old or congested wood at soil-level after flowering.
Propagation: During late autumn or early winter, take hardwood cuttings 25-30cm (10-12in) long and insert them in a nursery bed. They root quite easily and after only one season can be moved to their permanent positions in the garden.

Rosa rugosa

Ramanas Rose · Japanese Rose (UK)
Turkestan Rose · Japanese Rose (USA)

This hardy and sturdy deciduous shrub comes from Eastern Asia and has established itself as one of the best-known species roses. It is handsome, with hairy and prickly shoots and wrinkled dark green leaves, glossy above but downy beneath. During mid-summer it develops moderately-scented solitary flowers up to 7.5cm (3in) wide. Flowering often continues intermittently into autumn. It is then that the bright red tomato-shaped fruits, or 'hips', appear. Several red and pink-flowered forms are available, such as 'Frau Dagmar Hastrup' (single, pale rose-pink flowers, vivid pink in bud, with cream stamens); 'Rubra' (single and magenta-red); 'Roseraie de L'Hay' (often sold as 'Plena', bearing large, double, crimson-purple flowers with cream stamens); and 'Scabrosa' (large, single, violet-crimson flowers).
Height: 1.5-2.1m (5-7ft)
Spread: 1.2-1.3m (4-4½ft)
Cultivation: Ordinary well-drained garden soil is ideal, beware of sandy, chalky or very heavy clay soils. An open position in full sun or light shade is suitable, but avoid heavily shaded areas. Very little pruning is needed. If bushes do become overcrowded, cut them back in spring.
Propagation: Detach sucker-like growths in autumn, planting in a nursery bed. Alternatively, take hardwood cuttings 23cm (9in) long in autumn and insert them in sand-lined trenches in a nursery border.

Left: **Rosa rugosa 'Frau Dagmar Hastrup'**
This reliable species rose develops single, pale rose-pink flowers with cream stamens during mid-summer and intermittently through to autumn. These are followed by bright red, tomato-shaped fruits, commonly called 'hips' or 'heps'.

Ribes sanguineum 'Brocklebankii' with its golden-yellow foliage is a useful slow-growing and smaller form. It contrasts perfectly with the purple-leaved Smoke Tree *Cotinus coggygria* 'Foliis Purpureis'

Rosa rugosa is superb as a hedge, especially when peeping over a low brick wall. The wall also helps to prevent rubbish from the road collecting around the hedge's base. Set the plants 75-90cm (2½-3ft) apart.

TREES AND SHRUBS

Right: **Viburnum x bodnantense**
This impressive, sweetly-scented, winter-flowering deciduous shrub is a welcome addition to any garden. Several shrub forms are available, with flowers appearing on naked branches during winter.

Viburnum x bodnantense

A well-known, slow-growing deciduous shrub with dull green, toothed leaves, tinged bronze when young. The sweetly-scented, densely-packed, 2.5-5cm (1-2in) long clusters of rose-flushed white flowers appear on naked branches during mid-winter. It is available in several forms, including 'Dawn', with large clusters of richly-scented flowers, and 'Deben', with scented white flowers, delightfully pink when in bud and opening from late autumn to spring. Another winter-flowering viburnum is the deciduous *V. farreri*, often better known as *V. fragrans*. The highly scented nature of its pink-tinged white flowers is indicated by its synonym. From early winter to early spring it reveals its flowers in pendant clusters 2.5-4cm (1-1½in) long. For slightly later scented flowers *V. carlesii* 'Aurora' with pale pink flowers — but red in bud — and 'Diana' with red buds that open to reveal pink flowers are well worth considering.
Height: 2.7-3.5m (9-12ft)
Spread: 2.4-3m (8-10ft)
Cultivation: Well-drained but moisture-retentive soil is best; add well-decomposed compost, leaf-mould or peat if drainage is poor. A sunny position suits it best. Very little pruning is needed, other than the occasional removal of weak or old branches. Cutting back such shoots encourages the development of fresh shoots from the plant's base.
Propagation: During late summer, low-growing branches can be layered: this is the easiest method of increasing the plant for the home gardener.

Viburnum x bodnantense is best sited by a path or near the house if the highly-scented winter flowers are to be fully appreciated. Add an underplanting of spring bulbs to create extra and continuing colour.

Weigela Hybrids

These are some of the most beautiful of all hardy shrubs, with 2.5-3cm (1-1 ¼ in) long, rather honeysuckle-shaped flowers during late spring and early summer. They are the result of crossing *Weigela florida* with other Asiatic types. Many named forms are available, such as 'Abel Carriere' (deep rose-carmine with a yellow throat), 'Ballet' (dark pinkish-red), 'Bristol Ruby' (bright ruby-red with near black buds), 'Eva Rathke' (bright red), 'Fairy' (soft rose-pink), 'Newport Red' (dark red) and 'Styriaca' (red buds opening to reveal pink flowers). Weigela was formerly known as Diervilla, when the genus was named in honour of the Frenchman Dierville. In many old books it is mentioned under this name.

Height: 1.5-1.8m (5-6ft)
Spread: 1.5-2.4m (5-8ft)
Cultivation: Well-drained but moisture-retentive rich soil and a position in full sun suit it best. It requires regular pruning, each year after flowering, cutting back one or two of the old stems to soil-level. This will encourage the development of fresh main shoots from ground-level.
Propagation: Take hardwood cuttings 25-30cm (10-12in) long in mid to late autumn and insert them in a nursery bed. Rooting takes about a year. Alternatively, during mid-summer, take 7.5-10cm (3-4in) long half-ripe cuttings from non-flowering shoots and insert them in pots of equal parts peat and sharp sand kept at 16°C (61°F). Pot up the cuttings when rooted and slowly harden them off. Place them in a cold frame during winter and plant them out into a nursery bed in spring. They will need to remain there for about a year before being set in their permanent positions.

Left: **Weigela 'Bristol Ruby'**
This is one of the many hybrid weigelas, previously often known as Diervilla. *It does best when planted in rich, moist soil and given a sunny position.*

Further plants to consider

Aesculus x camea
Red Horse Chestnut (UK and USA)

Height: 4.5-6m (15-20ft)   Spread: 2.4-3m (8-10ft)
A beautiful chestnut with mid-green leaves and 15-20cm (6-8in) high candles of rose-pink flowers in early to mid-summer.

Erica herbacea
Erica carnea

A well-known hardy evergreen sub-shrub with several pink and red forms. These include 'Adrienne Duncan' (carmine-red), 'Eileen Porter' (carmine-red), 'Myretoun Ruby' (deep rose-pink), 'Praecox Rubra' (deep rose-red), 'Springwood Pink' (rose-pink) and 'Winter Beauty' (rose-pink).

Lilac — Garden Forms

These are the forms of the Common Lilac (Syringa vulgaris) with large heads of flowers. Many have pink or red flowers, and include 'Congo' (scented, dark red in bud and becoming pink), 'Marechal Foch' (single, carmine-rose), 'Mrs Edward Harding' (claret-red), 'Sensation' (purplish-red) and 'Souvenir de Louis Spaeth' (wine-red).

Malus floribunda
Height: 3.5-4.5m (12-15ft)   Spread: 3-4.5m (10-15ft)
A well-known round-headed hardy deciduous tree with single bright carmine flowers fading to pink in early summer.

Malus x eleyi
Height: 6-7.5m (20-25ft)   Spread: 4.5-6m (15-20ft)
A hardy deciduous spring-flowering tree with single reddish-purple flowers. These are followed by similarly coloured fruits.

Prunus dulcis 'Rosea-plena'

Height: 5.4-7.5m (18-25ft)   Spread: 5.4-7.5m (18-25ft)
This double pink-flowered form of the Common Almond is a delight in late spring.

Tamarix tetrandra
Tamarisk (UK and USA)

Height: 3-4.5m (10-15ft)   Spread: 3-4.5m (10-15ft)
A large, feathery and wispy hardy deciduous flowering shrub with pale to mid-green leaves and bright pink flowers in early summer. It is an excellent plant for coastal areas.

Weigelas suit a mixed border, or one filled by shrubs and small trees with underplantings of bulbs. The form 'Foliis Purpureis', with purple leaves and pink flowers, creates long-term interest.

INDEX

COMMON NAMES

Names set in *italic* type are those used in North America

INDEX

LATIN NAMES

CREDITS

Photographers
The majority of the photographs in this book have been taken by Eric Crichton © Salamander Books Ltd.
Copyright in the following photographs belongs to the suppliers:
Pat Brindley: 33 (Top)
Eric Crichton: 19, 26/27, 29 (Top), 37 (Bottom), 53, 82 (Left), 82 (Left), 84, 88 (Top), 90 (Bottom)
Ralph Gould: 29 (Bottom)
Peter McHoy: 14/15, 68/69
David Squire: Front Cover, 6, 7, 10/11, 11, 18/19, 24,25, 31, 48/49, 62, 63, 65 (Top), 66 (Centre), 70/71, 73 (Top), 73 (Bottom), 74 (Bottom), 76/77, 78, 78/79, 82 (Right), 83 (Top), 84/85, 85, 86, Back Cover.

Artists
Copyright of the artwork illustrations on the pages following the artists' names is the property of Salamander Books Ltd.
Nicki Kemball: 6/7, 12/13
Steve Linds (Linden Artists): 8, 8/9, 9, 10, 11
Clive Spong (Linden Artists): Front and Back Covers

Editorial Assistance
Proofreading and indexing by Joanna Chapman

PRINTED IN BELGIUM BY

proost
INTERNATIONAL BOOK PRODUCTION